Hosanna!

ST. PAUL'S EPISCOPAL CHURCH
P. O. Box 753
Port Townsend, WA 98368

By the author

Grandfather Clock and Other Finger Plays, Word Rhymes and Action Rhymes

Joyous Days: A Collection of Advent and Christmas Activities

Hosanna!

Calendars, Creative Projects, and Crafts for Lent and Easter

Sharon Lee

1817

Harper & Row, Publishers, San Francisco

Cambridge, Hagerstown, New York, Philadelphia, Washington
London, Mexico City, São Paulo, Singapore, Sydney

Grateful acknowledgment is given for use of the following: "Body Joy," "Communion Joy," "Calvary," and "Where is the Lord?" reprinted by permission from *Rainbow of Seasons* by Sharon Lee. Copyright ©1983 by Augsburg Publishing House. "Hosanna!" and "I Can Sing" reprinted by permission from *Hosanna Song Book* by Sharon Lee. Copyright ©1977 by Augsburg Publishing House.

 For information address Harper & Row, Publishers, Inc., 10 East 53rd Street, New York, N.Y. 10022. Published simultaneously in Canada by Fitzhenry & Whiteside, Limited, Toronto.

88 89 90 91 92 10 9 8 7 6 5 4 3 2 1

Contents

Introduction

I have two vivid memories of the Good Fridays of my childhood. One is standing in my little white junior choir robe, along with the other children of Mt. Carmel Lutheran Church in Milwaukee, Wisconsin, in the shape of a human cross as we sang, "Beneath the Cross of Jesus." Sometime between the hours of twelve and three on each Good Friday afternoon of our elementary school years, we would serve as a musical bridge between sermons on "The Seven Last Words of Christ." It was a serious day and even at ages seven or eight, we knew it.

The other memory is at home with my family a few years later when societal realities had changed the Good Friday worship hour to evening. The hours of twelve to three were, in our house, still serious—a time of remembering the gift of Jesus' life for us. We could read, my mother said, or just "do something quietly," but it was not a time for dodge ball or bike riding.

It is not the same in these days. What stores or businesses close Good Friday afternoon? And the ashes of Ash Wednesday on the foreheads of worshippers are not a sight our children will remember. No—the fact is Lent does not get big press today. Or even much acknowledgment in this latter part of the twentieth century A.D.

Hosanna! is written to help Christians keep the seasons in these contemporary times. It is written for families. Many of these activities originated in our home: we still eat Holy Week dinners on our family-decorated Lenten tablecloth. It is written for church schools and Christian day schools, for youth events, retreats, nursery schools and day care centers, for learning centers, devotionals, and congregational worship services.

Here you will find Lent and Easter calendars, egg crafts and Easter cards, fingerplays and races, discussion ideas, word games, cooking activities, songs, action rhymes, puzzles, banners, material for a motion choir, decorations for the congregational Easter breakfast, a mini-movie, phrases to learn in "sign" (language of the hearing-impaired), a reader's theater, celebration crafts, patterns of crosses (nearly fifty), bells and butterflies, and a series of worship services for the Lenten season with an emphasis on outreach and sharing. And much more!

I hope you will find this a rich resource, one that reflects the beauty and depth of these two seasons. Even in our world, Lent can be a time of thoughtfulness, of personal reflection and meditation. Perhaps, *especially* in our harried age, does the annual Lenten season provide a needed time for renewed prayer and preparing—in ourselves and in our world—for the exultation and celebration of Easter, of Jesus' death and Resurrection.

God's gift is wondrous, indeed. Let us rejoice! Hosanna!

How to Use Hosanna!

The crafts, activities, and projects in this Lent/Easter collection are coded by grade level to aid you in selecting appropriate activities for your class or family. The codes are in parentheses following the craft title. You will note that many activities span several levels in both ability and interest. Following is a key to the age-level codes.

P preschool and kindergarten
L lower elementary—grades 1–3
U upper elementary—grades 4–6
J junior high—grades 7–8
S senior high—grades 9–12
A adult

Indexes to Activities by Age Level

Activities without Age-Range Designations

Activities for Age-Level "P"

Activities for Age-Level "L"

Activities for Age-Level "U"

Activities for Age-Level "J"

Activities for Age-Level "S"

Activities for Age "A"

PART ONE
LENT

Introduction to Lent

Lent is the quiet time of the Christian year. It is the solemn season following the starlight of Epiphany and leading to the sunrise of Easter.

Lent is not twilight or dusk. It is pre-dawn . . . at the end of the darkness. If Easter is the season of God and Pentecost, the season of the Spirit, Lent is the season of the Son.

These forty days (in which Sundays are not counted) are symbolic of Jesus' forty days of testing in the wilderness—a time of prayer and fasting before his earthly ministry began.

In ancient times, Lent was the period of instruction and penance—a preparation time for baptism on Easter Eve. It was the season of good works, especially prayer, fasting, and the giving of alms. In our day, it is still a special time to cleanse ourselves and to share with others, a time to contemplate and examine, but not to withdraw. It is a time to strive for purity and holiness, for the goodness taught and lived by the Lamb of God "who has taken away the sins of the world."

If Christmas is the season of hope, and Easter the season of joy, Lent is the season of faith.

Healing will come . . . believe it.

Forgiveness awaits . . . believe it.

Reconciliation is ours . . . believe it.

This is the season to accept God's grade and to extend it into the world.

It is in the days of Lent we best "do justice . . . love kindness and walk humbly with our God." (Micah 6:8b) Know that the steps we walk are steps on the path to Easter morn.

Calendars and Crafts

Lenten Calendars

Here are several calendar ideas to mark the six weeks of this special season leading to the glory of the Easter Resurrection. These might be used as a project for the whole class or each student may have one calendar to complete week by week. They are also very appropriate for a family experience!

Symbol Poster Calendar

(L/U/J)

Materials
- poster paper
- ruler
- marking pens
- colored paper (optional)
- scissors (optional)

Draw lines with a ruler to divide a large piece of poster paper into uneven sections. Add a large new Lenten symbol (cut from colored paper or colored with marking pens) to one section each week until all six sections are filled. Possible Lenten symbols include palm branches, donkey, bread and wine, money bags, crown of thorns, sword, rooster, rock, and cross nails.

Prayer Wheel Calendar

(P/L/U/J/S)

Materials:
- poster paper
- ruler (or a straight edge)
- marking pen or crayon
- pretzel knots (the curved kind)
- old magazines (optional)
- scissors (optional)
- glue (optional)

Draw an 8½-inch-diameter circle on a piece of poster paper and divide the circle into six sections. Each week in the Lenten season, write a new prayer for a group or person in one of the sections, or glue in a picture of your prayer subject. Glue a real pretzel to each section as the prayer is completed. (Explain that the pretzel was a symbol to early Christians of praying arms.)

The teacher may write the prayer for the very youngest children or let them simply use pictures. Prayer subjects might include the elderly, the congregation, the world situation, your family, and so forth. You could use pictures from old magazines.

Butterfly Scenes Calendar

(L/U)

Materials:
- poster paper
- scissors
- pencil
- marking pens
- glue

Draw a large butterfly on a piece of poster paper and cut the shape out twice. On *one* of the butterflies, cut three irregular shapes in each wing, being careful to leave them attached on one edge (you will be creating six flaps, or doors). Place this butterfly on top of the other one, folding back the flaps and tracing the cut-out shapes onto that butterfly.

Glue or draw six pictures of scenes from the Passion story (see p. 25 for suggestions), one on each of the shapes you've traced on the uncut butterfly.

On the cut butterfly, fold the flaps closed again and decorate the doors with marking pens. Glue this colorful butterfly poster into place on the other butterfly.

Each Sunday in Lent, a new door will be opened to show a Lenten picture.

Cross Strip Calendar

(L/U/J/S)

Materials:
- felt or burlap
- scissors
- glue
- felt, colored paper, or fabric pieces
- dowel

Cut a strip of felt or burlap approximately 6 inches wide and 36 to 42 inches long. If you use burlap, fringe about 1 inch on the bottom. Glue a different form of the cross (see p. 81 for ideas) on the strip each week in Lent. Use felt, colored paper, or other fabric for the cross material. Fold over the top 1 or 1½ inches and glue it down for a hanging hem. Slip a dowel through the hem.

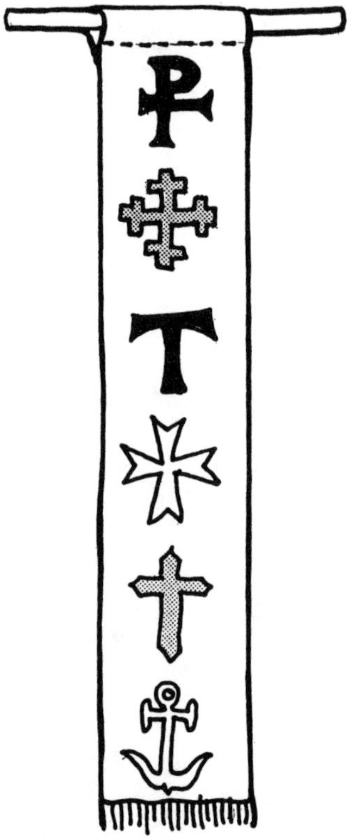

Passion Picture Calendar

(L/U)

Materials:
- poster paper
- ruler
- marking pens
- scissors
- glue or staples and stapler

Cut six squares of poster paper (8 by 8 inches is a good size). Each week in Lent, draw a different scene from the Passion story on one of the squares (see p.90 for ideas for the scenes). When completed, glue or staple four of the pictures together vertically and glue or staple the remaining two onto the sides to form the arms of the cross-shaped calendar.

A Collection of Crosses

The cross is perhaps the most familiar Lenten symbol. Here is a variety of creative cross projects. See p.81 for a large number of cross shapes.

Laced Cross

(P/L)

Materials:
- cardboard or poster board
- hole puncher
- yard prepared wth liquid starch

Draw a cross shape on a piece of white or colored lightweight cardboard or poster board. Punch holes around the edges of the cross shape. Provide colored yarn with ends which have been dipped in liquid starch and dried.

Children may outline the cross by lacing the yarn in and out of the punched holes. Start and end on the back of the cardboard.

Mosaic Cross

(P/L/U)

Materials:
- construction paper
- glue
- tissue paper (optional)
- dyed eggshell pieces (optional)

Draw an outline of a cross on black or white construction paper. Tear lavender or black construction or tissue paper into small pieces. The student may glue the pieces on within the outline of the cross.

Option:
Dyed eggshell pieces (soaked previously in food coloring—mix blue and red for purple or use Easter-egg dye) may also be glued within the cross outline to create a textured mosaic.

Sprayed Cross

(L/U)

Materials:
- cardboard or poster paper
- scissors
- gold or silver spray paint

Cut a cross shape out of cardboard or poster paper. Spray it with the color of gold or silver, precious metals often used for royal crowns, as a sign of Jesus' kingship.

Clay Cross

(L/U/J)

Materials:
- clay
- rolling pin
- foil
- table knife
- pencil
- toothpicks (optional)
- tempera paint (optional)

Prepare clay recipe given below. Roll out the clay on foil. Cut a cross shape out of the clay with a table knife, poke a hole at the top with a pencil, and allow the cross to dry.

When the cross is dry, push a leather strip, ribbon, or yarn through the hole to serve as a necklace chain.

Option:
You may etch symbols or words on the cross while clay is still wet. Use a toothpick for clear clean lines. When the cross is dry, you can paint what you've etched, or even the whole cross, with tempera paint.

CLAY

Mix 1 lb. of baking soda, 1 cup of cornstarch, and 1¼ cups of water in a pan. Cook over low heat until it forms a doughlike substance. Allow to cool.

Worship Cross

(L/U/J)

Materials:
- wood
- nails
- hammer

The class may nail two pieces of wood together to form a simple, crude cross. This may be used as a processional cross in the worship service each Sunday during Lent.

Twig Crosses

(P/L)

Materials:
- tree twigs
- yarn
- scissors

Gather twigs or small branches 4 to 8 inches long. Form crosses with two twigs each. The children may wind yarn around where the sticks intersect until the cross is very stable. Black or purple (Lenten colors) would be very appropriate colors for the yarn.

These might be distributed to the congregation at the Good Friday or Ash Wednesday services.

"For Me" Cross Picture

(L/U)

Materials:
- colored construction paper
- scissors
- glue

Cut a tau cross out of colored construction paper. Glue it in the center of a piece of paper or poster board.

Note:
Use an interesting shape for your background paper—not just the traditional 8½-by-11 or 9-by-12-inch size. Try a triangle, circle, or tomb-shaped piece of paper. This will add more interest to the project and may also serve as a symbol background.

Write "Jesus died" on the cross. Cut out a doll figure for each member of your family and write the appropriate name on each figure: "for Mom," "for Shawn," "for Bryan," "for Dana," " for me." Glue the figures around the cross.

Straw-Painting Cross Tree

(L/U)

Materials:
- black tempera paint
- water
- construction paper
- newspaper or craft cloth
- straw
- scissors
- glue

Prepare tempera paint by thinning it with an equal amount of water. Lay the construction paper on newspaper or craft cloth to protect the surface you're working on.

Drop a small amount of paint in the middle of the piece of construction paper. Blow through a straw to move the paint around to form a tree with branches. Allow the paint to dry.

Cut small crosses out of construction paper and glue them to the tree branches.

Thumbprint Cross

(P/L/U)

Materials:
- paper
- ink pad
- marking pen

Draw an outline of one of the simpler cross shapes on a piece of plain paper. (See cross shape ideas, p. 81.) Children may fill in the cross with their thumbprints (using an ink pad for the print). Write "Jesus died for me" above or below the cross.

Class Cross Tree

(L/U/J/S)

Materials:
- fruit-tree branch (6 to 12 feet high)
- bucket or Christmas tree stand
- colored paper, fabric, styrofoam or balsam wood
- scissors
- yarn

Make various crosses (see p. 81 for ideas). Hang them on a 6-to-12-foot anchored tree. Add new crosses each week through the Lenten season. Possible materials for the crosses are colored paper, fabric, styrofoam, and balsam wood.

Note:
If you keep a fruit-tree branch in warm water through Lent, it will blossom with buds by Easter Sunday.

Cross Windows

(L/U/J)

Materials:
- black paper
- colored tissue paper
- scissors
- glue

Select a cross shape (see p. 81). Cut two of that shape out of black paper, and one out of colored tissue paper, ¼ to ½ inch smaller on all sides.

Cut the cross shape from inside the two black pieces, leaving ½-inch to 1-inch border around a hollow cross. Place the colored tissue cross between the two black crosses and glue all three together.

Jesus' death and Resurrection has burst through the darkness of sin. As Christians, we walk through Lent looking toward the light of Easter. Hang your crosses in a window during the Lenten season. Various classes in the church school may volunteer to decorate different windows in the building, so the church is filled with light streaming through the crosses during Lent.

More Lenten Crafts

Charcoal Pictures

(L/U/J/S)

Materials:
- paper
- charcoal sticks or wine corks and matches
- hair spray or other fixative

Use charcoal sticks (from an art supply store) or wine bottle corks burned black on one end. Draw a charcoal sketch of one of the scenes in the Passion story.

Spray with air spray to set the drawings.

Note:
This is a good activity to be done close to Ash Wednesday. Talk about the age-old custom of worshippers being marked with ashes on their foreheads on Ash Wednesday as a reminder of Christ's sacrificial death.

Prayer Tree

(L/U/J/S)

Materials:
- tree branch, anchored in pot or Christmas tree stand
- colored paper
- marking pens
- scissors

Lent is a special time of prayer. Ask the students to think of people or subjects for whom to pray (see Mt. 25:35-40 for ideas). Write prayer concerns on colored paper shaped like eggs. These might be hung from a large fruit-tree branch displayed in a corner of the sanctuary where all congregation members may add prayer concerns throughout Lent.

Chalice/Bread Impressions

(P/L/U)

Materials:
- patterns
- cardboard
- scissors
- white or pastel paper
- color crayons

Cut the chalice and bread patterns (p. 82) from cardboard. Place them under a piece of white or pastel paper. Color hard over the cardboard pieces, rubbing firmly until the shapes show through.

You might do several rubbings on each piece of paper, placing them in an interesting abstract design.

These might be matted and displayed in the narthex on Holy Thursday or during Holy Week.

Holy Week Scenes

(L/U)

Materials:
- styrofoam meat trays (various sizes and shapes)
- marking pens
- bible (optional)

Gather several sizes of styrofoam meat trays. Talk with the class about the various events and stories of Holy Week (see p. 89 for ideas). Ask each student to designate a scene he or she will illustrate (several may duplicate events if you have a large class.)

The students will draw the scene on the styrofoam trays. Marking pens work well and provide vivid colors. Students may wish to use Bibles for researching story details.

Several of the illustrations might be used to create a Lenten bulletin board.

Holy Week Etchings

(L/U)

Materials:
- paper plate
- crayon
- black tempera paint
- liquid detergent
- brush
- etching tool (ball-point pen or wooden skewer)

With a crayon, heavily and completely color one side of a paper plate. Mix black tempera paint with a small amount of liquid detergent and brush this mixture over the colored paper plate. Allow it to dry. When completely dry, scratch a Holy Week scene or design on the plate, exposing the crayon underneath. An old ball-point pen or wooden skewer makes a good etching tool.

Burlap Painted Pictures

(P/L/U)

Materials:
- burlap pieces
- cardboard
- stapler
- tempera paint and brushes

Staple pieces of burlap to cardboard backing. Mix tempera paint a bit thicker than usual. The children may paint a Lenten scene on the burlap. Allow to dry.

The texture of this completed project is very interesting.

Torn Paper Calvary Scenes

(L/U/J/S)

Materials:
- colored paper
- glue

Tear colored paper into shapes to create a Calvary picture

Note:
There is something about the technique of tearing which frees amateur artists to risk their own creativity. There are not the same expectations as when they wield a paintbrush, crayon, marker, or scissors.

The picture might include the three crosses, the hill, clouds, a path, crowds, a tree or two, rocks—whatever comes to the imaginative mind.

Good preparation, such as telling or reading the crucifixion story, will greatly enhance this activity.

Mini-Movie

(L/U/J)

Materials:
- envelope
- scissors
- paper strip
- marking pens

Use a small or business-size envelope. Cut a window in the front, seal the flap and cut off the two ends. Cut a strip of paper just large enough to slip through the envelope.

Draw pictures the size of the window to illustrate one of the stories in the Lenten season. Glue these, in order, on the paper strip. Pull the story-strip through the envelope as you tell the story which appears in the window.

Egg Crafts

For centuries, the egg has been the symbol of the Resurrection—of hope and new life. Before the Reformation, eggs were blessed in the churches at Easter celebrations. They were not to be eaten then, but instead given as gifts to friends and family.

Today, they are perhaps our most familiar and common household reminder of the most miraculous of all events: the dawn of new life for all humankind.

To Prepare Eggshells

Use eggs which are room temperature. Poke holes in both ends—pierce the yolk with a darning or other large needle. Shake vigorously, covering both ends. Blow through the smaller hole so that the egg white will come out the larger hole.

Rinse shell well with water (inside and out). Handle the shell carefully as you work with it, as it is light and fragile. Dry with tissue or soft towel.

Note:
Jumbo chicken eggs or duck eggs (if available) are a nice large size for craft activities.

Flower Eggs

(L/U/J)

Materials:
- prepared or hard-cooked eggs
- tempera or poster paints
- cotton swabs (Q-tips are a common brand)
- shallow bowls (one per color)
- hair spray or fixative

Prepare eggs as directed above or use hard-cooked eggs. Pour a small amount of paint in shallow bowl. Dip a cotton swab into the paint until it is full of paint. Press the side of the swab against the egg to create a petal. Keep adding petals until you form a flower.

Add dots or wavy lines for extra trim. When using several colors, use a different swab for each color.

Allow the designs to dry. Spray with hair spray or other fixative.

Colorful Yarn Eggs

(L/U/J)

Materials:
- eggs
- paper and pencil (for design sample)
- knitting yarn
- rubber cement or glue

This is a popular craft in Poland.

Prepare the eggs as directed earlier. Design a pattern on an egg-shaped piece of paper, deciding how many colors of yarn to use and how to place them.

Working on one section at a time, apply rubber cement or a craft glue to the egg. Wrap or apply the yarn as indicated on your pencil pattern. The yarn may be wrapped around, glued in swirls or circles . . . the possibilities are practically unlimited. Keep working until the entire egg is covered with yarn.

Note:
It is usually best to work from the ends toward the middle of the egg. Use plenty of yarn, gluing each strand close to the one before so that no part of the egg shows through.

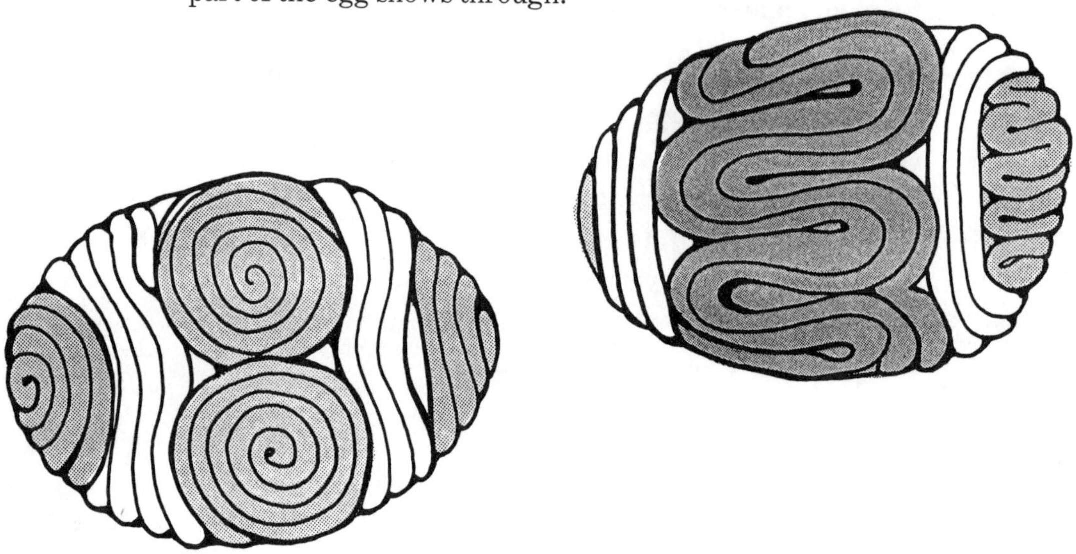

Painted Eggs

(U/J/S)

Materials:
- eggs
- rubber band (fairly wide)
- pencil
- fine paintbrush and paint or fine-line marking pens
- fixative

Prepare the eggs as indicated previously. Draw a band around each egg, either lengthwise or crosswise. (Use a wide rubber band as your guide to pencil in the lines.) This line around the egg represents eternal life. It is always used in the eggs decorated in the countries where egg painting has become a sophisticated art: Poland, Ukrania, Romania, Czechoslovakia.

Continue decorating the egg with your choice of designs. Flowers and nature symbols are commonly used. You will become more skilled with each egg you do.

First draw the outline of a symbol and then fill it in with color to obtain the best form. Use a very fine paintbrush and paint, or fine-line marking pens; either way, use bright colors! These are not the pastel Easter eggs we are familiar with in our culture; they are rich, deep, carefully decorated eggs. Spray when dry.

Picture Eggs

(L/U)

Materials:
- prepared eggs
- picture materials (cards, catalogs, seals, stickers, etc.)
- scissors
- glue
- colorless nail polish
- egg carton cups (optional)

Use prepared eggs. Cut out small pictures from gift wrap, greeting cards, magazines, nursery catalogs (flowers, etc.), or old Sunday school curriculum, or use seals and stickers. Glue carefully onto eggshells.

When glue has dried, paint the picture area with colorless nail polish. This is an excellent fixative which also adds strength to the eggshell.

Note:
These eggs might be attached to individual egg carton cups with a drop or two of glue in the bottom of the carton. Each child may take an egg home as his/her Egg Picture Story. These, of course, would be the ones with pictures relating to the Lent or Easter events.

Egg People

(L/U/J)

Materials:
- hard-cooked eggs
- marking pens
- other materials (yarn, colored paper, fabric scraps, etc.)
- scissors
- glue
- egg carton cups

Use hard-cooked eggs, as these eggs will require a lot of handling. Create characters from the Passion story using marking pens, yarn, colored paper, fabric scraps, etc. Arrange in individual egg carton cups. These might even be arranged in groups with surrounding twigs as trees, background scene, or any other set you might design.

Possible subjects: Pilate, Jesus, disciples, Mary, Caiphas, Pilate's wife, soldiers.

Possible scenes (with several characters): the Last Supper, the prayer in the garden with the sleeping disciples, the arrest in the garden, Peter's denial. Small signs in front might identify scene and/or characters.

Note:
These would be nice fresh decorations for the annual congregational Easter breakfast!

Egg Basket

(U)

Materials:
- eggs
- manicure scissors
- paint
- glue
- ribbon (each piece ¼ inch wide and 5 to 7 inches long)
- bow (optional)
- articles to fill, such as Easter grass, Easter cookies, flowers (optional)

Begin with plain eggs. Crack each one in half, leaving one half of the egg shell a bit larger than the other. (Use the eggs for scrambling.) Cut each larger eggshell half evenly around the broken edge, using manicure scissors. These might be prepared before the class begins, although the children could easily do this if you have enough small scissors.

Paint the eggshell basket with a favorite color, inside and out. Use spray paint or a cotton swab dipped in paint, supporting the egg with a straight pin through the bottom of the shell, attached to a block of styrofoam. When the paint has dried, spray with a fixative.

Glue a ribbon across the top of the egg to form a handle, and another ribbon around the top edge of the basket, covering the handle ends. Add a small bow, if you like, where the ribbon ends meet.

Fill the basket with Easter grass and a verse on a miniature card, or a special Easter cookie. You might also choose to fill it with small artificial flowers in a nice arrangement as a special gift.

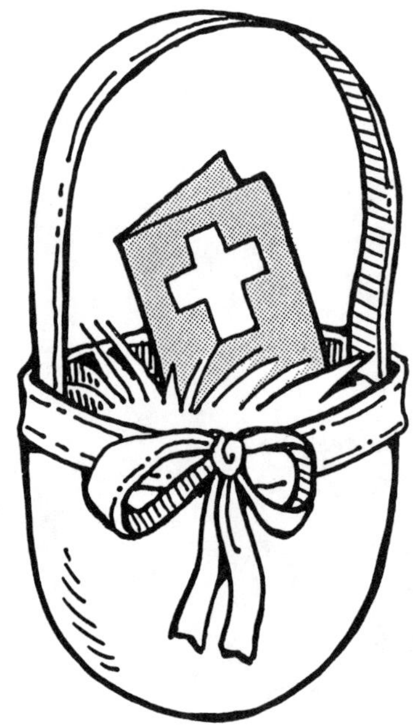

Easter Vases

(L/U)

Materials:
- eggs
- manicure scissors
- nail polish or hobby enamel
- wooden curtain rings (1 to 1½ inches diameter)
- artificial flowers
- Easter grass (optional—may help hold flower display upright)

These are sweet gifts for a special sweet person!

Decide which type of vase you wish to make (or make one of each). The horizontal egg vase must be prepared by cutting away an oval opening on the side of the egg. (The inside will make great omelettes.)

The vertical egg vase will have a fairly small opening (the top quarter of the egg) cut away.

Paint the egg vase with pretty-colored nail polish or bright enamel from a hobby shop. Let it dry. Glue the dried egg vase onto a wooden curtain ring for a base. Fill with tiny artificial flowers. Present with a smile!

Word Songs, Finger Plays, Action Rhymes, Word Games, and Creative Writing

Word Songs, Finger Plays, and Action Rhymes

Word songs are words said in rhythm without music. They bring a sense of oneness to the group doing them, a delight in the beat together, yet they do not require the skills of music reading or singing. They are within the reach of every child. They bring a sense of achievement and they're fun! These word songs are in 4/4 time. The dots indicate the beats.

Hosanna (For Palm Sunday)

(P/L)

Fetch a donkey
(running in place)
Hurry up, hurry up
(roll hands around each other)
Spread your cloaks on the ground (rest)
(perform that motion)
Jesus will come like a king today
(look in distance)
Hear the Hosanna sound! (rest)
(hands cupped to ear)
Second time through: half the class will say "Hosanna" over and over while other half repeats above verse.

Palm Sunday

(P/L)

Stretch up high to wave your palms
(stretch up)
Bend down low to adore him
(bend down)
Today Jesus enters the town like a king
(one hand move with fingers walking)
And the cheers of the crowds are for him.
(other hand open and close several times)

Last Supper

(L/U/J/S/A)

(Pass a cup around the circle of participants as this is said)

Twelve disciples
Pass the cup
Blessed are you
With him to sup.

Pass the wine
Share the bread
"Remember me,"
Is what he said.

Communion Joy

(U/J/S/A)

Joy is the bread
Joy is the wine.
Joy is to know
That the gift is mine.
(Repeat, growing softer)

Calvary

(P/L/U)

Once on a hill
(form hill shape with one hand)
Called Calvary,
Jesus died
(make cross with two fingers)
On a cross for me.

Crucifixion

(U/J/S/A)

(These words are meant to be said quietly as a group)

He died on Good Friday
On Calvary's hill.
The cross said, "I love you,"
And is saying it still.

Hosanna!

Sharon Lee

Jesus, Lamb of God

Sharon Lee

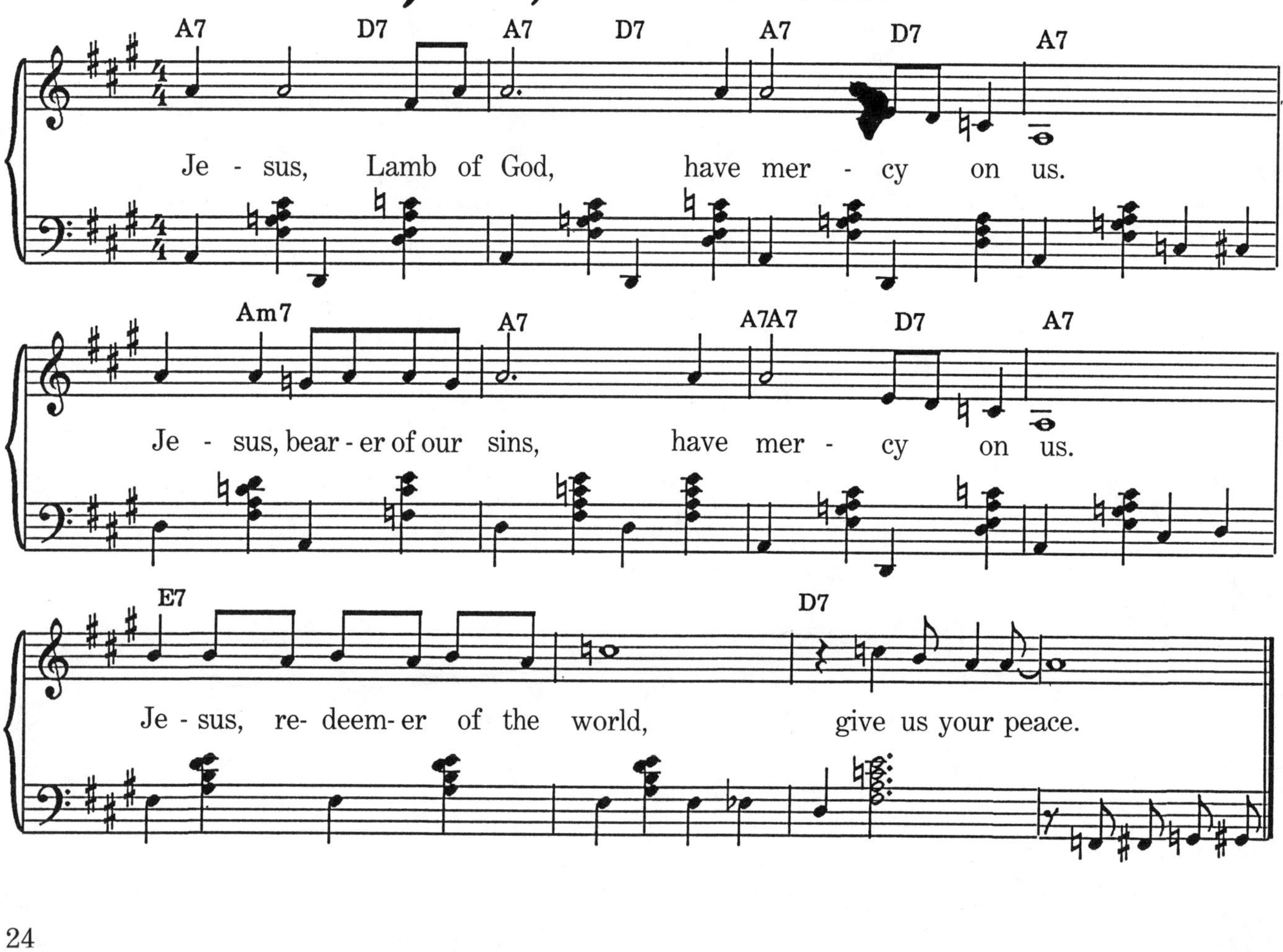

Word Games

People and Places of The Passion

(U/J/S/A)

Match the people and places on the left with the correct descriptions on the right. There are two separate sets to try.

1. Gethsemane	a. he denied his friend 3 times
2. Caiphas	b. the thief let loose by the crowd
3. Judas	c. he carried the Lord's cross
4. Peter	d. she first saw him alive!
5. Barrabas	e. he offered his burial place to the Christ
6. the upper room	f. he was given the care of Jesus' mother
7. Simon of Cyrene	g. his kiss betrayed his master
8. John	h. place of the Last Supper
9. Joseph of Arimathea	i. high priest who charged "Blasphemy"
10. Mary Magdalene	j. Jesus' prayer place

Just for added challenge, there are two extra items in the right column

11. Pilate	k. the hill of the crucifixion
12. first thief	l. saved at the last minute
13. Peter, James, and John	m. they gambled for his garments
14. Calvary	n. he ridiculed Jesus and dared him to escape
15. Pilate's wife	o. a king's parade
16. second thief	p. victim of a bad dream
17. Roman soldiers	q. crowned King of the Jews
18. Jesus Christ	r. they stole the thirty pieces of silver
19. Palm Sunday	s. they slept during Jesus' prayers
20. vinegar	t. the Roman governor who tried to wash his hands of it all
	u. she washed Jesus' feet at her brother's home
	v. drink on the cross.

Lent Long-Distance Lines (a telephone quiz)

(U/J)

Each telephone number on the dial also contains letters. Here's an exercise in deduction and investigation! Choose one of the letters from the circle of each number given and put them all together (one from each number circle) to make the name of a person or object connected with the Passion story.

For example—Number 3 would give you a choice of D, E, or F. Number 8 would offer T, U, or V. Number 6 would let you choose M, N, or O. So 3-8-6 would ultimately create—F-U-N! Hope that's what you have doing this challenging quiz!

1. 6-2-7-9 (a name)
2. 5-6-4-6 (a name)
3. 7-3-8-3-7 (a name)
4. 5-4-6-4 (a title)
5. 2-7-6-7-7 (an object)
6. 9-4-6-3- (an object)
7. 2-4-7-4-7-8 (a name)
8. 7-2-5-6 (an object)
9. 2-7-3-2-3 (an object)
10. 2-7-6-9-6 (an object)

Lent Word Find

(U/J/S/A)

Can you find the words below in the cross?

Jesus
Good Friday
John
Peter
James
redeem
God
betray
deny
garden
trial
thief
hope
Savior
love
Last Supper
Calvary
Gethsemane
cross
bread
wine
king
Hosanna
palm
pray
Judas

Look up and down, forward and backward and diagonally (up and down).

S U S E J
K L X Y F
F D N C T
P E T E R
D R H G E
K L A T D
H R T U M N E D R A G F Y E L V R G F E I H T
O M D L A S T S U P P E R E F E H R N H O J Q
P X A Z J U D A S L S V A M V S J I H I L B M
E P Q Y R O I V A S E X V O E G W U A D K H P
K O B L M
Y J R A E
A C J C H
R B V T G
T A U R O
E F K I O
B R E A D
L P N L F
H T A H R
O B M F I
S K E L D
A N S C A
N D H N Y
N P T R G
P Z E I J
E B G O D

Lent Word Find (key)

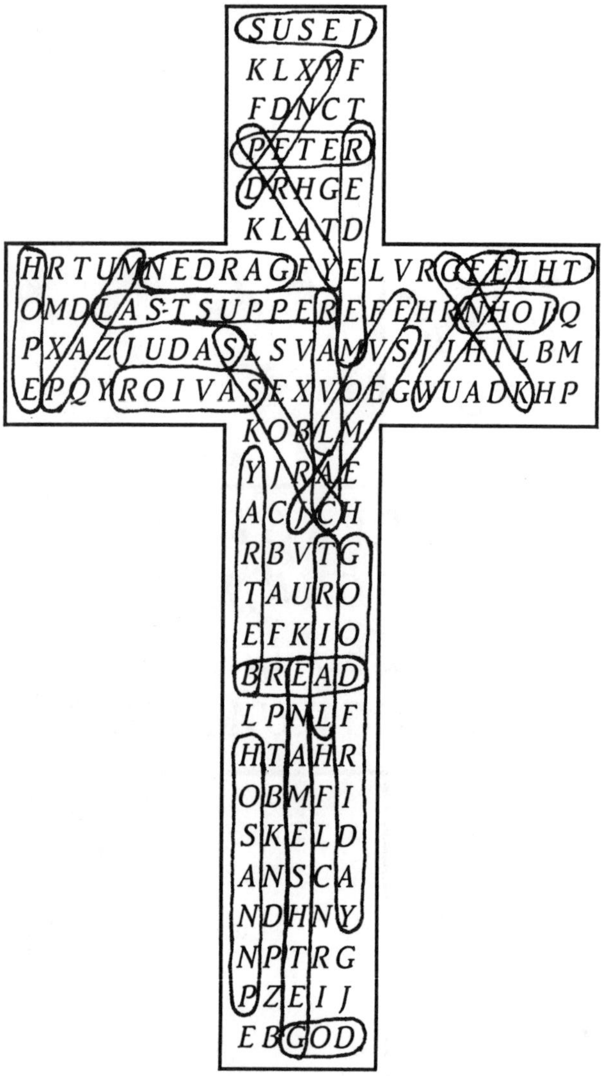

Lent Long-Distance Lines (a telephone quiz) (key)

1. M-A-R-Y
2. J-O-H-N
3. P-E-T-E-R
4. K-I-N-G
5. C-R-O-S-S
6. W-I-N-E
7. C-H-R-I-S-T
8. P-A-L-M
9. B-R-E-A-D
10. C-R-O-W-N

People and Places of The Passion (key)

1. j.
2. i.
3. g.
4. a.
5. b.
6. h.
7. c.
8. f.
9. e.
10. d.
11. t.
12. n.
13. s.
14. k.
15. p.
16. l.
17. m.
18. q.
19. o.
20. v.

r and u are extra

"People of the Passion" Puzzle

(U/J)

Can you find the names of seven people from the Passion story in the squares below? You may start anywhere and move in any direction, following the lines. Sometimes one letter in the diagram is used more than once in one name.

Here's a clue or two: There are four disciples. There is one public official. There is a good friend. There is the hero of the story.

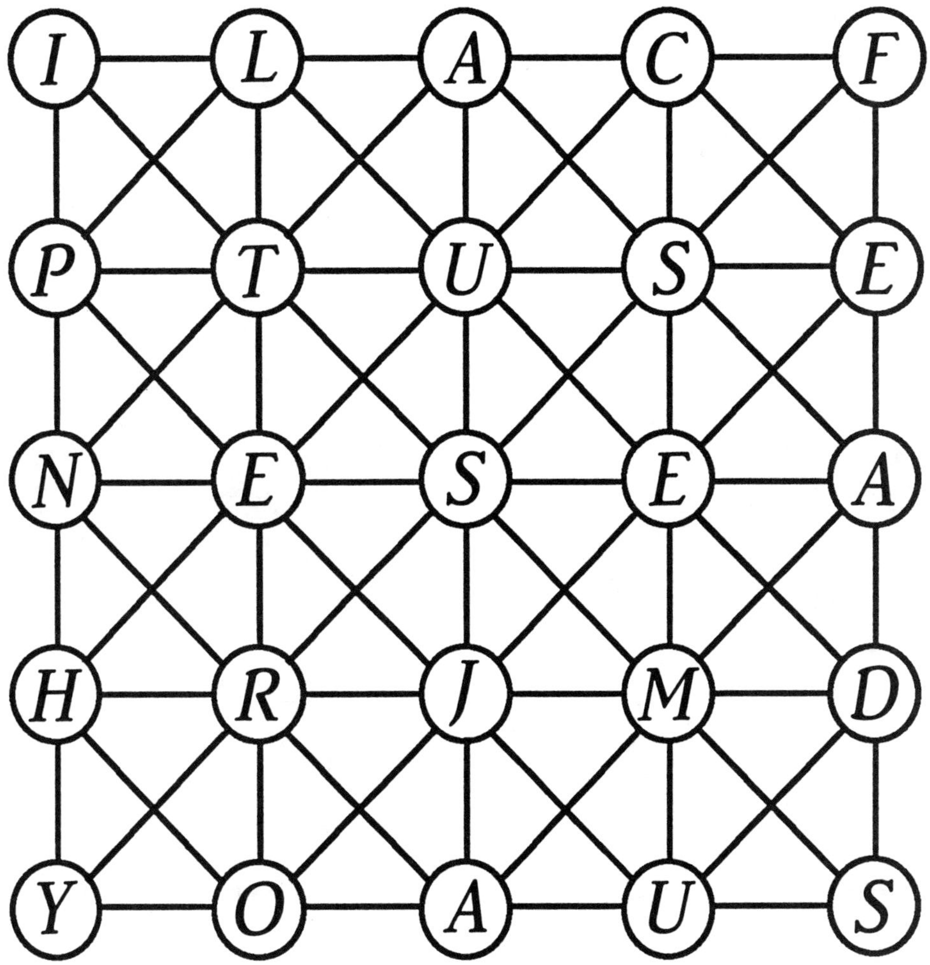

"People of The Passion" Puzzle

(Key 1) JUDAS

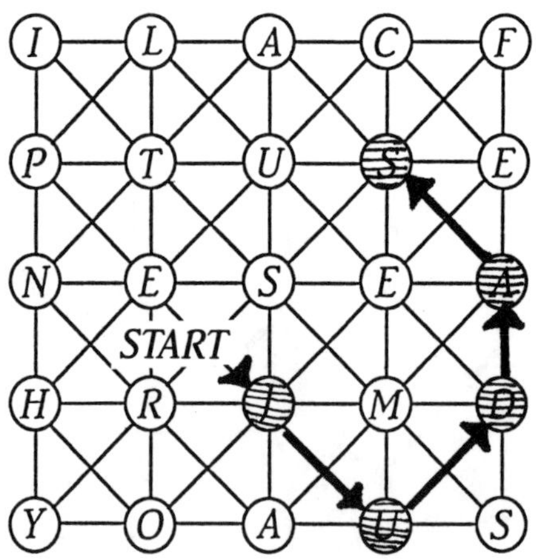

(Key 2) JOHN

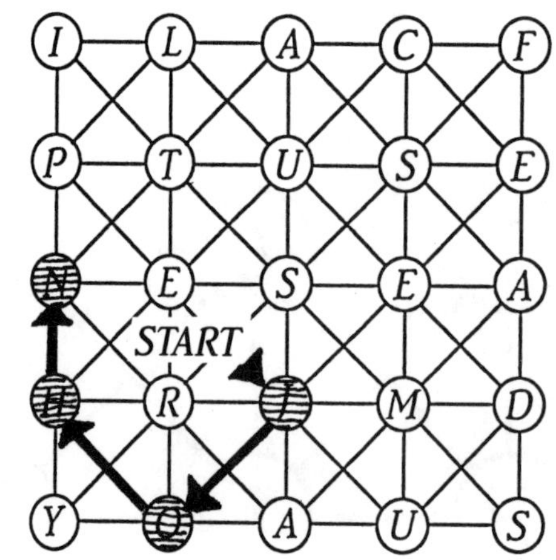

(Key 3) JAMES

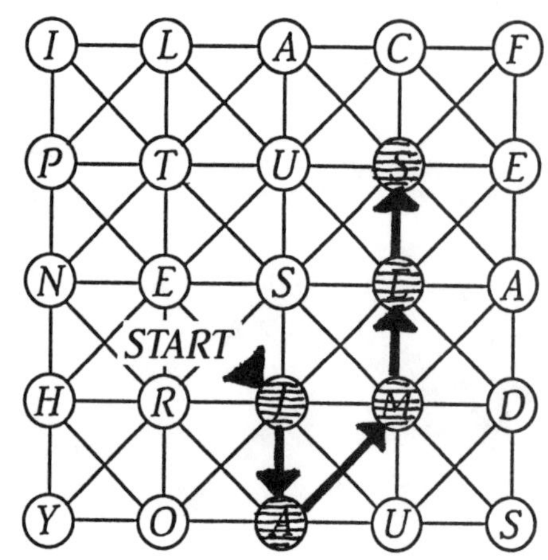

(Key 4) PETER

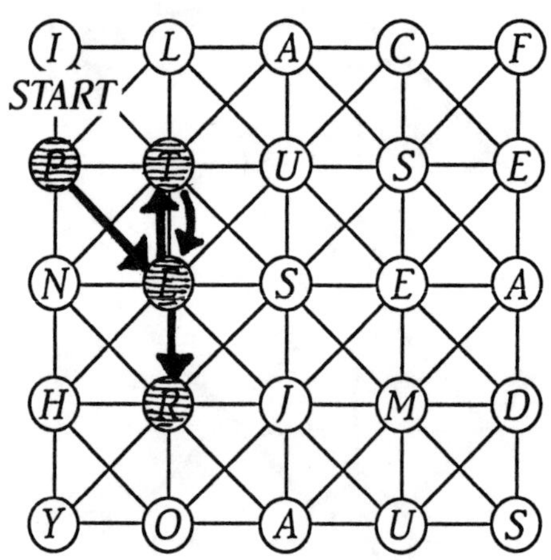

(Key 5) PILATE

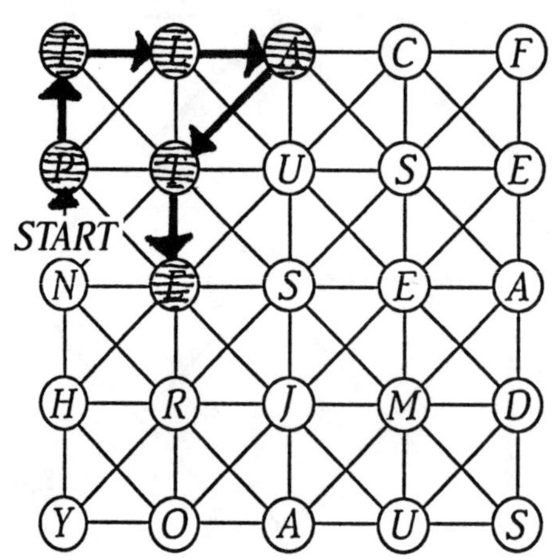

(Key 6) MARY

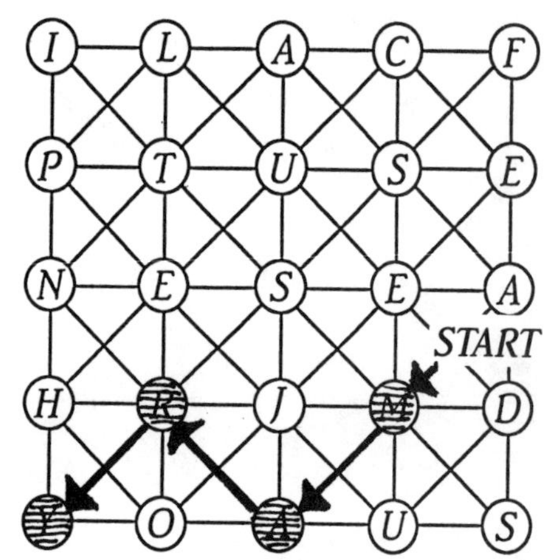

(Key 7) JESUS

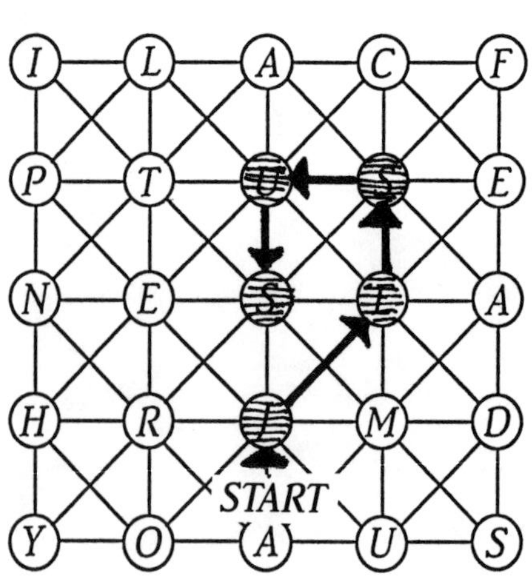

Creative Writing

Let the spirit and the feelings of the Lenten season speak through your own words. Here are several ideas to spark your creativity!

A Lent People Poem

(U/J/S/A)

This poetic form, the cinquain, may be written by individuals or by the whole class together. The name "cinquain" comes from the five-line structure ("cinq" is the French word for "five").

line 1 one noun (the name of a Lent character)

line 2 two adjectives (words describing person in line 1)

line 3 three "ing" verbs (also referring to person in line 1)

line 4 four feeling words about the person—four individual words or a four-word phrase

line 5 one noun meaning the same as the word in line 1

Example:

PETER
confused, alone
denying, rejecting, hiding
afraid to get involved
deserter

Skinny Poem

(U/J/S/A)

Choose an event or person in the Passion story. Write a poem of few words on that subject.

Here's the structure:

1 word (title)

3 words* (*this will be the same phrase repeated 3 times in the poem)

2 words

4 words

3 words*

7 words

2 words

4 words

3 words*

1 word

You will have a total of 30 words in your poem.

VERSION FOR LENT

Mary
Blessed among women
Chosen one
How could you know?
Blessed among women.
Should the angel have told you then?
Prophesied this?
Death on a cross?
Blessed among women,
Weep.

VERSION FOR EASTER

Mary
Blessed among women
Chosen one.
How could you know?
Blessed among women.
Should the angel have told you then?
Prophesied this?
Death on a cross?
Blessed among women,
Wait!

Poem Pictures

(U/J/S)

Choose phrases from the gospels telling of the Passion story and illustrate those lines with original or magazine pictures. An example might be Luke 23:34, "Father, forgive them, for they know not what they do." (see pg.90 for other ideas). The pictures may well be contemporary visualizations of the events, or you may draw historical depictions of the scenes.

Display these pictures with the appropriate verses written as free-verse poems. This could become an annual Lenten Art show in your church.

Cross Names

(L/U/J/S/A)

Do you have a cross name? Do your first and last names have letters in common? Use your middle name if necessary! Print your name intersecting on the common letter to form a cross. Now print it with the names going in the other direction.

```
       B              J
    J a m e s         a
       n              m
       n            B e n n i s
       i              s
       s
```

Riddle Writing

(L/U)

Make up a three- or four-line riddle about a character in the Passion story. Say one line at a time, while the others try to guess your riddles as soon as possible.

Example:

I have four feet.
I worked on a Sunday.
I carried a king.
Who am I?

(Answer: the Palm Sunday donkey)

Discussion Ideas and Group Activities

Discussion Ideas

Starters/ Finishers

(U/J/S/A)

Materials:
- paper
- pencil

Ask the students to write down their own beginning or end to a statement you will make. They may then share their answers in small groups or with a partner. You may hear some of the thoughts in the whole class setting, too.

Note:
This is a technique to involve all the students. Their writing an answer down means *everyone* has something to share—not just the usual class leaders.

Some ideas for Starters/Finishers Statements

1. ________________ is my favorite name for Jesus.
2. If I could ask Jesus about anything, I'd ask him ________________.
3. During Holy Week, Jesus was not human when ________________.
4. During Holy Week, Jesus was most divine when ________________.
5. ________________ was the most terrible day of Holy Week.
6. Jesus, himself, must have been most disappointed Holy Week when __.
7. In the whole Passion story, I can empathize most with ______ (person).
8. In the whole Passion story, I can relate most closely with __ (a person).

Choices

(L/U/J/S/A)

Everyone will move to the center of the class space. The leader will read a statement with two choices, indicating a different side of the area for the participants to move to, according to which choice they make for each statement.

Each side may talk together about why they made their choice—then the two sides might discuss their selections. Usually the leader can just step back and let the discussion flow.

Note:
The center is off bounds; everyone must make one choice or the other.

Some ideas for Choices:

1. I would rather have been at the Palm Sunday Parade/Last Supper.
2. My faith is more like Good Friday/Easter.
3. On Tuesday of Holy Week, Jesus taught the people two commandments:
   1) Love the Lord with all your heart, soul, and mind.
   2) Love your neighbor as yourself.

   Which commandment do you think our society keeps best?
4. Which commandment is hardest for you to keep (see no. 3)?
5. My faith is like the sun/a tree.
6. Our world today is more like Thomas the Doubter/Peter the Denier.
7. I think of Jesus more often as a healer/teacher.
8. I need Jesus more as a healer/teacher.
9. My faith is more like spring flowers/autumn leaves.

Group Activities

Passion Story Ranking

(U/J/S/A)

Divide the class into groups of three to five people. Ask each group to rank these six Passion characters in order by amount of guilt:

Peter
Barrabas
Judas
Pontius Pilate
the crowd
Caiphas

Rank the characters from 1 to 6. Each group must reach a consensus.

Bring the groups together and write their rankings on a blackboard or newsprint pad. Then stand back and let the groups at each other!

Being There Cross

(U/J/S)

Materials:
- poster paper
- marking pens

Divide the class into groups of two to four people. Each group will draw a cross like the one sketched here, and choose a scene of the Passion story—for example, Palm Sunday, the garden of Gethsemane, the Last Supper in the upper room, Calvary. Imagining themselves there, they will fill out the five sections of their cross.

This is best done on a large piece of poster paper.

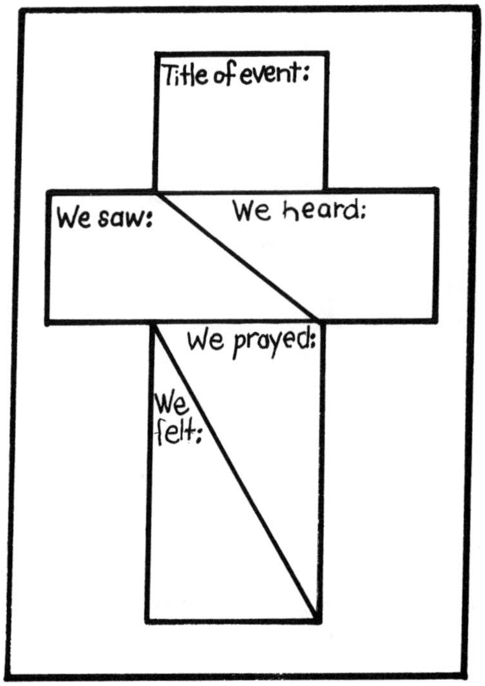

Reader's Theater

(U/J/S)

Read the story of Peter's denial (Mark 14:66-72). Assign characters: Peter, the maid, bystander, Jesus, narrator. You may wish to record your reading on a cassette tape, complete with introduction and background music.

See p. 90 for subjects for other Lent playreadings.

Note:
Check that all participants have the same bible version.

Holy Week Tableau

(L/U/J/S)

Decide on Holy Week scenes to portray. Select characters for each. Choose costuming if you desire. Post yourselves in a frozen scene (this is what a tableau is). Have someone take polaroid pictures or slides of each tableau.

Put the tableaux together with scripture and/or music.

Option:
You may decide to choose one event and have it shot from different angles, focused on different characters, etc. The Last Supper, for example, would be a good one for this treatment—pictures of the bread and wine, of individual disciples, of Jesus and Judas, of Judas alone, of several disciples watching Jesus, hands passing bread, etc.

"Signs" of Lent

Learn these Lenten phrases in sign language, the form of communication used by many hearing-impaired people.

(L/U/J/S)

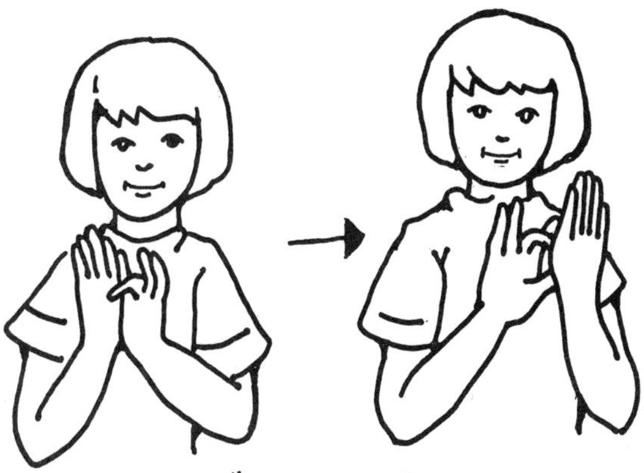

"Jesus"

"Jesus" Touch the middle finger of each hand to the palm of the other hand, right finger to left palm and then left finger to right palm *(this signifies touching the nail wounds in Jesus' palms).*

"Is"

"Lord"

"Is" Raise the index finger of one hand and move it from lips forward.

"Lord" Lift index finger and thumb to form an L. Draw from left shoulder down across body to right hip as if drawing a sash.

"Praise"

"Him"

"Praise" Clap hands and lift both hands back with palms forward.

"Him" Point one index finger upward.

Kyrie *for a* *Motion Choir*

(L/U/J/S)

The following might be performed in a number of ways by a motion choir or a group of children.

Lord, have mercy upon us
(slowly raise head and both hands in unison)
Christ, have mercy upon us
(lower head while slowly moving arms out to sides)
Lord, have mercy upon us.
(slowly extend hands forward to front while facing forward)

Option 1:
The whole choir may perform the Kyrie with motions straight through.

Option 2:
Divide the choir into three groups. Each may say one line only, and all hold their pose until the end.

Option 3:
Do Option 1 together, then begin Option 2, each group repeating its own words and actions several times.
(This is in canon, like a round.)

This experience may be a part of the congregational worship service or the Sunday school worship, or used simply as a class experience.

Lent Song Story

(U/J/S)

Select a melody for your song, for example "Kum ba Yah" or "Praise and Thanksgiving."

Divide the class into groups of three or four. Each group will write a verse for the song story about its assigned Holy Week event. Possible subjects are Palm Sunday parade, Last Supper, prayer in the garden, Jesus' arrest and trial, crucifixion. You may also decide to add an Easter verse.

All verses will be written to fit the selected melody.

Print the words of all the verses on newsprint or poster board. Sing the whole song together as a class.

Class Prayer Cross

(P/L/U/J)

Each week during Lent, at the beginning or end of the class session, the students may all stand in the shape of a cross for the prayer.

Class Lent Poster

(U/J)

Materials:
- poster paper
- scissors
- colored paper
- clear contact paper
- tape

Use a piece of poster paper for background. Each student will cut out a cross shape (see p. 81 for ideas) and print his/her name on that cross. Glue those to the background poster. The teacher will print **JESUS** in outline letters on a sheet of clear contact paper. Tape that over the crosses.

Use this poster to teach that Jesus' death covers our sins.

Holy Week Puzzles

(U/J)

Materials:
- cards (3-by-5 or 5-by-7-inch)
- marking pens
- scissors

Choose several events of the Passion Week story (see p. 89 for ideas). Use one 3-by-5 or 5-by-7-inch card for each event. Draw a wavy or jagged line down the center of each card.

On the right side, neatly print the name of the event. On the left side, draw an illustration of that event, using marking pens.

Cut each card on the drawn line. Mix them up, then match the titles and the pictures of the Holy Week events.

Lent Montage For Today

(U/J/S)

Materials:
- newsprint or poster paper
- marking pen
- magazines
- scissors
- glue

Use newsprint or poster paper for background. Write title (see below for ideas) across the top or to one side. Students will cut out pictures from magazines to illustrate the title. These may be glued on in a random manner. Cover the paper with pictures.

Possible Lent titles:

"Father, forgive them for they know not what they do."

"You will deny me."

"As you did it to one of the least of them, you did it to me." (Or same phrase, inserting "not.")

Sponge Garden

(P/L/U)

Materials:
- container
- sponge (3 to 5 inch diameter)
- seeds (flowers or herbs)

Soak a sponge (3 to 5 inches in diameter) in water; squeeze well. Place in a dish or shallow bowl. Choose seeds to plant. These may be small flowers, herbs such as chives, dill or parsley, or even clover seeds. Insert them into the open pores of the sponge. Water the sponge sparingly—just enough to keep it damp—and keep it in a warm, shady place. When the seeds begin to sprout, place the dish with the sponge garden in a sunny spot.

Lent/Easter Alphabet

(U/J/S)

Materials:
- old white window shade
- marking pens

Unroll an old white window shade. Print all the letters of the alphabet along the left side, using various colored marking pens. Hang the shade somewhere in the class area. Through the Lenten season, the students may write words or phrases beginning with each letter which are appropriate to this and the Easter seasons. There may be as many words listed for each letter as the students can think of.

Some Lent/Easter Words

A—Ash Wednesday, Arrest, Allelulia, Annas

B—Bread, Body and Blood, Betrayer

C—Crown, Caiphas, Crucifixion, Cross, Christ, Cup

D—Disciple, Denial, Doubter

E—Easter, "Eloi, Eloi"

F—Feast of the Passover

G—Golgotha, Gethsemane, Garden

H—Hosanna, High priest, "Hail Master"

I—Inri (Jesus of Nazareth, king of the Jews), Iscariot

J—Judas, Joseph of Arimathea

K—King of the Jews

L—Linen, Last Supper, Lord

M—Mount of Olives, Mary, Messiah

N—Nails

O—Olives (Mt. of)

P—Palm Sunday, Passover Supper, Pontius Pilate, Peter

Q—Quake

R—Roman centurion, Resurrection, Rex (king in Latin)

S—Simon Peter, Simon of Cyrene, Sepulchre

T—Trial, Thief, Thorns, Tomb, Thomas

U—Upper room, Unleavened bread

V—Vinegar

W—Wine

X— Chi Rho (Jesus Christ in Greek)

Y—"You will be with me in Paradise"

Z—Zebedee (father of James and John)

Color the Crosses

(P/L/U)

Cross—orange
Background—yellow

Cross—purple
Background—red

Cross—blue
Background—green

Cross—red
Background—black

Cross—white
Background—black

Color the Crosses Key

1. Trefoil cross—The three points on the ends represent the Trinity. The orange and yellow are sunrise colors signifying Easter morning.

2. Chi Rho cross—This cross is the most ancient sign for Jesus Christ, made from the Greek letters for Jesus and Christ. The purple represents Jesus' kingship and the red his role as Savior.

3. Cross of St. Andrew—Tradition says the apostle Andrew asked to be crucified on this form of the cross so that it not be like his Master's. The blue and green are colors of the created world in which Jesus lived and taught with his disciples.

4. Maltese cross—This historical cross goes back to the Crusades when the Order of Hospitallers, whose headquarters was on the island of Malta, used it as their emblem. It represents four spearheads, their points at the center. The red and black were colors often used on flags during the Crusade era.

5. Eastern cross—The top bar was the place for the inscription over Jesus' head. The bottom slanted bar was the Savior's footrest. The Eastern Church believes Jesus was crucified with his feet side by side not crossed as depicted by the Western Church. The white symbolizes Jesus' purity, the black sin (and also the color of the raiments worn by the priest in the Eastern Church during Lent).

Worship Services

Worship Services for the Six Sundays in Lent

The brief services contain the following worship elements for each Sunday:

Opening Devotional Prayer –
repeated each of the six weeks so the children may learn it.

Lenten Hymn ("Were You There") –
a new verse is sung every week, following the story of the Passion.

***JESUS' WORDS –**
this familiar passage is repeated each week. The phrase focused on each Sunday serves to introduce the specific gift giving for that week. The scripture reference is Mt. 25:37-40.

***Gift Giving –**
this is an offering time for that week, an opportunity for the participants to share during this special season. During the offering, the week's focus phrase will be added to the Jesus' Words Poster.**

Prayer –
the prayer relates to the focus for the day. If the two preceding elements are not a part of your worship, the prayer may still be acceptable—or you may choose to write your own prayer.

Psalm Verse –
These six verses are all taken from a group referred to as the Penitential Psalms, which were historically significant to Christians during the Lenten season. The children might be encouraged to learn the verse each week.

Closing Song –
the children will learn this song during the season.

**These might be optional for your situation. The other five elements can combine to create a full worship experience by themselves.*

***The Jesus' Words Poster will build during the six weeks of Lent. Each separate phrase may be written on a section of poster board and displayed. Example: Week 1*

I was hungry *and you gave me food*

Worship Service for The First Sunday in Lent

All: Come inside my heart today,
Help me share your love, I pray.

Hymn: Were you there when they crucified my Lord?
(repeat)
Oh, sometimes it causes me to tremble, tremble, tremble.
Were you there when they crucified my Lord?

Leader: Read Mt. 25:37-40.

Giving: Display Sign 1: "I was hungry and you gave me food." The children may bring cans of food to the front to place on the altar, in baskets, or stacked on the floor. If instructions to bring food have not been given the week before, a few teachers might bring up their food offerings and the students may bring theirs the next week.
(Music of "Were you there?" may be played softly during this offering time.)

Leader: Let us pray.
Generous Father,
You have filled our world with such good things. We thank you. Be with those who do not have enough to eat. Teach us to see and help them. Amen.

All: "You are my God, teach me to do your will," Ps. 143:10a.

Song:

African Melody, Words by Sharon Lee

Worship Service for the Second Sunday in Lent

All: Come inside my heart today,
Help me share your love, I pray.

Hymn: Were you there in the garden when he prayed?
(repeat)
Oh, sometimes it causes me to tremble, tremble, tremble.
Were you there in the garden when he prayed?

Leader: Read Mt. 25:37-40.

Giving: Display Sign 2. "I was thirsty and you gave me drink." The children may bring forward cans or envelopes of juice or other beverages.
(Play music of above hymn softly)

Leader: Let us pray.
Kind Creator,
Fill us with the rich rivers of your never-ending love. Help us to fill those who are in need of earthly food and drink. Amen.

All: "I lift my hands to you in prayer; like dry ground my soul is thirsty for you." Ps. 143:6.

Song: He died for me,
He died for me.
Jesus is Lord,
And he died for me.

Worship Service for the Third Sunday in Lent

All: Come inside my heart today,
Help me share your love, I pray.

Hymn: Were you there when the crowd called, "Crucify"?
(repeat)
Oh, sometimes it causes me to tremble, tremble, tremble.
Were you there when the crowd called "Crucify"?

Leader: Read Mt. 25:37-40.

Giving: Display Sign 3. "I was a stranger and you welcomed me." The children may bring forward the name of a new resident or new friend (on a slip of paper) whom they promise to pray for and make welcome during this season.

Leader: Let us pray.
God of care and love,
We know there is no time you go away. Thank you for being close to every one of us always. Help us to share your warm, deep love with others. Help us to be good friends. Amen.

All: "My trust is in you, O Lord; you are my God." Ps. 31:14.

Song: He died for me,
He died for me.
Jesus is Lord,
And he died for me.

Worship Service for the Fourth Sunday in Lent

All: Come inside my heart today,
Help me share your love, I pray.

Hymn: Were you there when they nailed him to the tree?
(repeat)
Oh, sometimes it causes me to tremble, tremble, tremble.
Were you there when they nailed him to the tree?

Leader: Read Mt. 25:37-40.

Giving: Display Sign 4. "I was naked and you clothed me." The children may bring forward articles of clothing they have brought for distribution to those in need.
(Play above music softly)

Leader: Let us pray.
Heavenly Father,
You see all that is good and all that is sinful in us, your children . . . and still you love us. Help us to be forgiving and loving, too. Amen.

All: "Remove my sin, and I will be clean; wash me, and I will be whiter than snow." Ps. 51:7.

Song: He died for me,
He died for me.
Jesus is Lord,
And he died for me.

I know he cares,
I know he cares,
I know he cares
For he died for me.

Worship Service for the Fifth Sunday in Lent

All: Come inside my heart today,
Help me share your love, I pray.

Hymn: Were you there when the world was dark and sad?
(repeat)
Oh, sometimes it causes me to tremble, tremble, tremble.
Were you there when the world was dark and sad?

Leader: Read Mt. 25:37-40.

Giving: Display Sign 5: "I was sick and you visited me." The classes may bring forward one of the gift projects* they have completed.
(Music may be played softly)

Leader: Let us pray.
Holy Comforter,
You bless us with life, with health and with energy. Thank you for these wonderful everyday joys. Help those who now need your healing power. Give them strength and help them to keep their strong faith and trust. Amen.

All: "I cried to you for help, O Lord, my God, and you healed me." Ps. 30:2.

Song: He died for me,
He died for me.
Jesus is Lord,
And he died for me.

I know he cares,
I know he cares,
I know he cares
For he died for me.

Worship Service for the Sixth Sunday in Lent

All: Come inside my heart today,
Help me share your love, I pray.

Hymn: Were you there when my Savior died for me??
(repeat)
Oh, sometimes it causes me to tremble, tremble, tremble.
Were you there when my Savior died for me?

Leader: Read Mt. 25:37-40.

Giving: Display Sign 6: "I was in prison and you came to me." The children may bring forward gifts of money for the purchase of books for a nearby prison or halfway house. Coordinate this with the appropriate officials.
(Music may be played softly)

Leader: Let us pray.
Gracious God,
You gave us the gift of your son that all our sins may be forgiven. Help us to show our love by living lives of forgiveness for others. Amen.

All: "I confessed my sins to you, and you forgave all my sins." Ps. 32:5.

Song: He died for me,
He died for me.
Jesus is Lord,
And he died for me.

I know he cares,
I know he cares,
I knew he cares
For he died for me.

**Possible gift projects:*

1. *"It only hurts when I laugh" book: glue cartoons the children have brought onto colored or white pages. Punch holes and assemble book with a yarn bow.*
2. *Packet of comfort verses: neatly print bible verses, one to each 3-by-5-inch card. The cards might be covered with clear contact paper. Tie cards together with a bright ribbon or yarn bow. Some possible verses are John 14:27, Ps. 3:20-22, Ps. 27:14, I Cor. 15:39-58.*

Possible recipients of gift projects are hospitalized church members, shut-in congregation members, children's hospital, and nursing home care units.

Cooking Activities

A Little Bit of Cooking in Lent

Hot Cross Buns

These Lenten treats have a history many centuries old. One story says that some 600 years ago, an English monk baked hot cross buns and gave them to the poor at Easter time. Cooks from then on have continued this season specialty.

The cross, made of white icing, is a reminder of the greatest gift ever given in human history: the life and death of God's own Son.

LENT HOT CROSS BUNS— a contemporary version

frozen bread dough (1 loaf)
currants or raisins (1/4 cup)
1 egg white, slightly beaten
powdered sugar (about 1 cup)
1/2 tsp. vanilla

Thaw bread dough. Add currants or raisins to dough. Roll into rectangle about 9 by 15 inches and cut 10 to 15 buns with a 2 1/2-inch biscuit cutter. Place buns on greased baking sheet. Let rise until doubled, about 1 1/2 hours.

With scissors, cut a shallow cross shape in the top of each bun. Brush each top with slightly beaten egg white. Bake in hot oven (400°) 12 to 15 minutes, until done and golden. Place buns on cooling racks.

Mix vanilla and remaining egg white with powdered sugar to icing consistency. Spoon icing into paper cone which has small tip cut off. Fill the cut crosses with icing while buns are still slightly warm.

Note:
The teacher may make the buns ahead of time and let class make icing and frost.

Pretzels—The Prayer Bread

Years ago, there were Christians who were not allowed to eat certain foods during the Lenten season. Among these forbidden foods were meat, milk, and eggs. Bread recipes ordinarily used milk and eggs, of course, so the bakers had to find some other way to make this important diet staple. The result was pretzels. Flour, salt, and water combined to make the dough which was rolled out and then shaped to resemble two arms in prayer. The German name for this bread was "brezel," which became "pretzel" in English. These snacks of our day are still a reminder of Lent as a season of deep and frequent prayer.

SOFT PRETZELS

1 cup warm water (105°–115°)
1 pkg. dry yeast
¼ cup sugar
1 tsp. salt
½ egg
2 Tbsp. softened margarine
3½–4 cups unsifted flour
1 egg yolk
1 Tbsp. water
coarse salt (often called kosher salt)

Dissolve yeast in the warm water. Add sugar, salt, egg, margarine, and 1½ cups of flour. Beat until smooth. Add enough additional flour to make the dough stiff. Cover bowl tightly with foil and refrigerate 2 hours or overnight.

Divide the chilled dough in half and place on floured board. Cut each half into eight equal pieces. Roll each piece into a braid about 18 to 20 inches long and shape each braid into a pretzel. Place on lightly greased baking sheet. Brush with egg yolk/water mixture. Sprinkle with coarse salt. Let rise in warm place until double, about 20 minutes. Bake in 400° oven about 15 minutes until done. Remove to cooling rack.

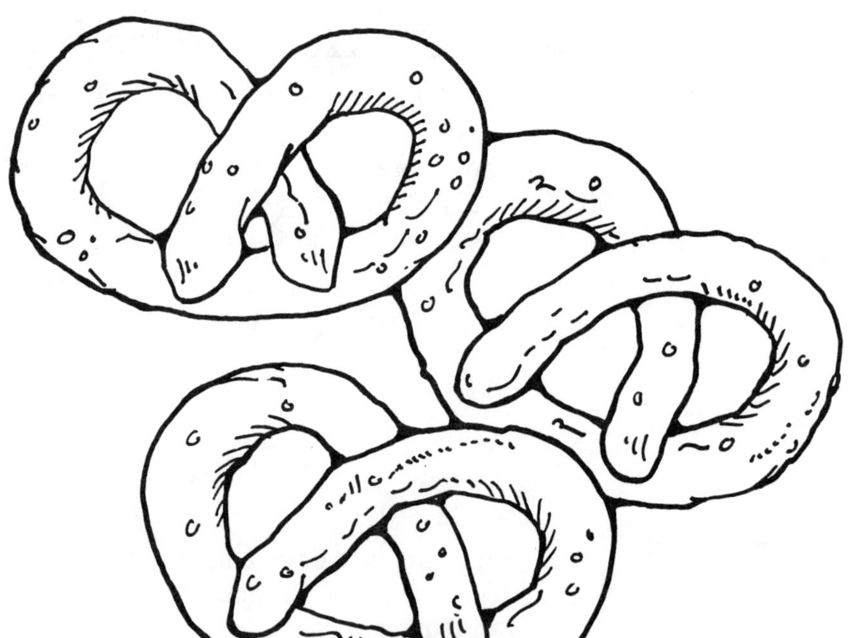

JUMBO BREAD STICKS

frozen bread dough (1 loaf), thawed (or an unsliced loaf of bread)
butter or margarine
your choice of garlic salt, celery salt, onion salt, poppy seeds, sesame seeds, or Parmesan cheese

Cut the thawed bread dough (or loaf) into sticks about 4 to 5 inches long by 1 inch thick. Dip each stick into melted butter and then place on greased baking sheet. Sprinkle bread sticks with your choice of above toppings. Bake in 375° oven for about 20 minutes, turning to brown evenly. Eat while still warm.

Note:
For very good, crispy bread sticks, place in pan of melted butter to bake, turning on all sides during baking time.

Irish Soda Bread

This is a tasty spring treat which might be made by the children during Holy Week classes or during children's time on Wednesday nights during the Lenten season. They might make several loaves to serve to the adults and children after a Lenten service.

IRISH SODA BREAD

4 cups flour
2 Tbsp. sugar
1 tsp. salt
2 tsp. baking powder
1 tsp. baking soda
2 Tbsp. caraway seeds
1 cup raisins
½ stick butter, melted and cooled
2 cups buttermilk
2 eggs

Mix all dry ingredients (the first seven ingredients) thoroughly. In another bowl, mix the butter, buttermilk, and eggs. Add this liquid mixture to dry ingredients and mix until dough is moistened. Turn dough onto floured board and knead until smooth.

Place the dough in a greased 9-inch poundcake pan. With scissors, cut a cross on the top. Bake in a 375° oven about 50 to 60 minutes, until done and golden. Cool on wire rack.

PART TWO
EASTER

Introduction to Easter

Easter is the Creator's party for all his children.

EASTER...

unexpected,
original,
God-planned,

the greatest, most spectacular, wonderful time the world has ever known!

EASTER is capital letters and exclamation points!!! A glorious tapestry of gold, orange, yellow, crimson, and brilliant, dazzling white light! Sunrise!

The story of Easter is the story of a marvelous, majestic early-morning miracle... a Risen Redeemer... God's Glorious Gift of eternal life to humankind.

EASTER is the Best Festival... the highest Holy Day.

Most of all, Easter is joy, joy, joy!

CHRIST IS RISEN
HE IS RISEN, INDEED!

"Let us, therefore, celebrate!" I Cor. 5:8a.

Calendars and Crafts

Ringing in Easter

Easter Bells

(P/L/U)

Materials:
- bell patterns
- marking pens
- scissors
- string
- stapler or glue

There is an Italian children's legend that all the church bells of the land fly to Rome each Maundy Thursday. There they make pilgrimages to the tombs of the apostles and sleep on the roof of beautiful St. Peter's Cathedral. Easter morning they all return to their own parishes to ring out the joyous news of Christ's resurrection!

Provide bell patterns (see p. 83) through the Easter season. As the children come into class each week, they may decorate a bell, cut it out, and add it to the string of bells. This string may run across the room or around the walls, along the hallway or wherever is most appropriate. By the end of the Easter season your area may be "ringing" with scores of Easter bells.

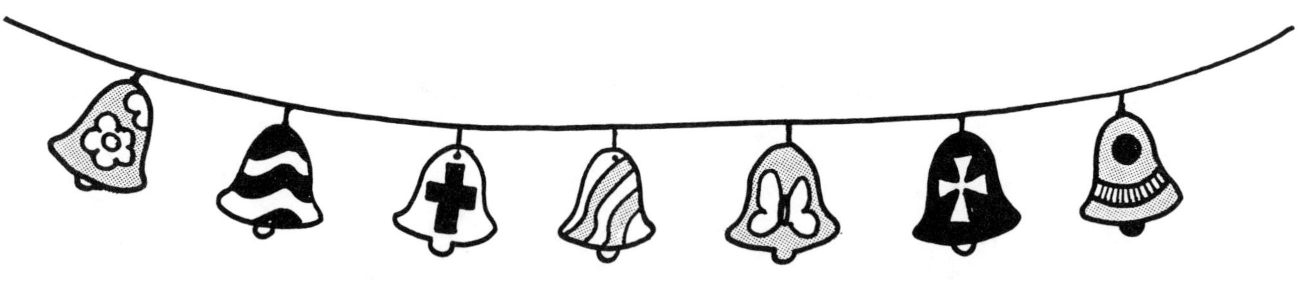

Easter Season Calendars

Butterfly Birth Calendar

(L/U)

Materials:
- poster paper
- colored paper (seven colors)
- scissors
- glue

Use a large sheet of poster paper for the background. Each week during the Easter season, cut a part of the butterfly out of colored paper and add it on as indicated in the illustration. Use seven different colors to highlight the explosion of this wonderful, joyful season.

Option:
These may be made as individual projects by each student on a smaller scale, perhaps on 9-by-12-inch background paper.

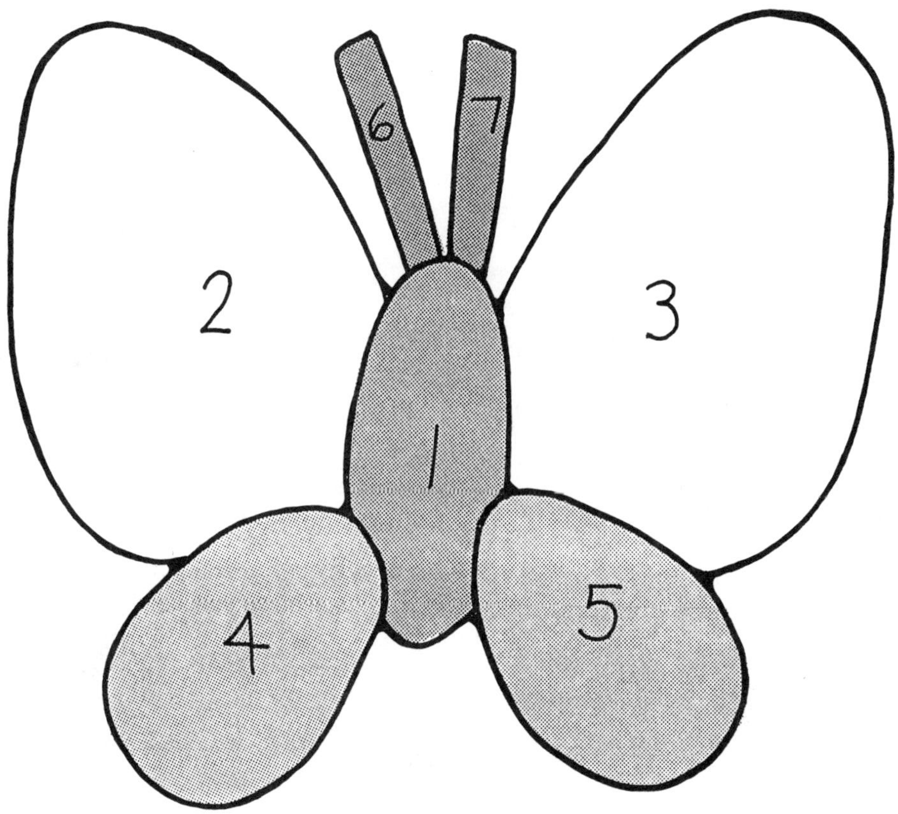

Butterfly Branches Calendar

(L/U)

Materials:
- poster paper
- marking pens
- scissors
- glue

Draw a tree branch on poster paper. On a separate piece of paper, draw a colorfully decorated butterfly to cut out and add to the tree each week in the Easter season. Marking pens add bright tones! See p. 84 for butterfly patterns.

Easter Mobile Calendar

(L/U)

Materials:
- poster paper
- scissors
- stapler or glue
- construction paper
- string
- scotch tape (optional)

Make a circle out of construction paper or poster paper (8 inches in diameter is a good size). Cut slit. Overlap edges and staple or glue together to form shallow cone. The symbols may be made of construction paper and attached to the rim of the cone-shaped base with string and scotch tape or staples. Thread a knotted string through the point of the cone and hang. You will add a new symbol each week to mark off the Easter season. Some Easter symbols to include: flower, star, baby chick, butterfly, sunrise, rainbow, and a crown.

Easter Path Calendar

(L/U)

Materials:
- poster paper
- marking pen
- tissue paper
- stapler
- glue
- button (optional)

Draw an outline of a tomb on the left side of a piece of poster paper. Print the words "HE LIVES" in the upper right quarter of the poster.

Each week during the Easter season, the students may add a colorful three-dimensional flower to the path leading from the tomb. The three-dimensional effect may be achieved by adding flowers on top of each other, each successively smaller.

Tissue paper of various colors for each flower (or even within one flower) would create a lovely effect. Staple the various flower layers together.

Option:
You may add a button center to the flowers.

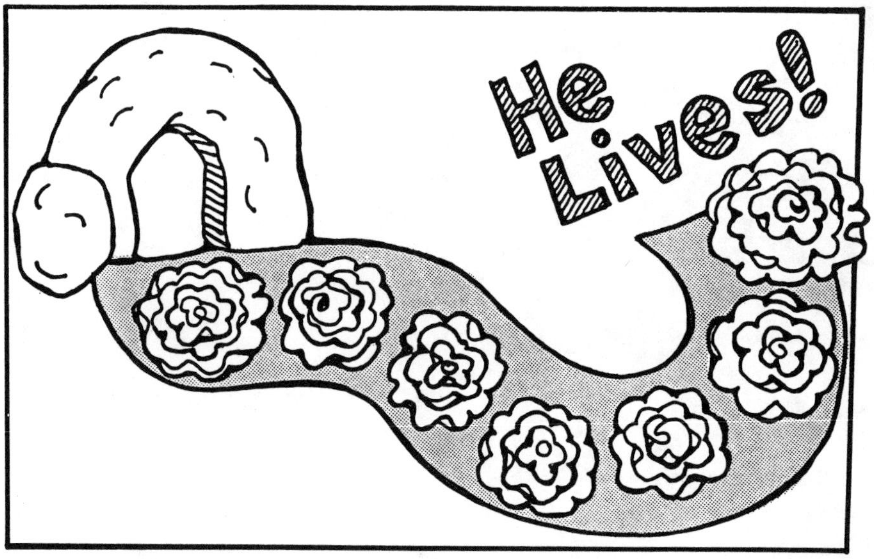

Beautiful Butterflies Picture Calendar

(P/L/U)

Materials:
- Beautiful Butterflies pictures
- marking pens or crayons

Provide a Beautiful Butterflies picture (see p. 85) for every student. Each week, the child will color the appropriate butterfly until, by the end of the Easter season, all seven are bright and beautiful.

Butterfly Wreath Calendar

(L/U)

Materials:
- poster paper or styrofoam
- butterflies (colored paper, tissue paper, or white paper)
- marking pens
- scissors and glue

Cut a wreath shape out of poster paper or styrofoam. Decorate a butterfly (see p. 84 for patterns) each week during the Easter season and add it to the wreath. The butterflies may be made of colored paper, tissue paper or white paper decorated with marking pens.

Easter Crafts

Butterfly Banner (may also be an Easter Calendar)

(U/J/S)

Materials:
- white or violet felt
- (18-24 inches by 24-36 inches)
- glue
- needle and thread
- stockings or cotton for stuffing
- purple felt
- sequins, braid, rickrack (optional)
- seven bible verses printed on paper
- dowel

Select a piece of white or violet felt, 18 to 24 inches by 24 to 36 inches. Sew or glue down a 1-inch hem across the top.

Cut two identical crosses out of purple felt. Sew together and stuff the crosses. Use old stockings or cotton for the stuffing—the crosses should not be very thick. Glue or pin the crosses onto the top two-thirds of the felt background piece.

Attach a strip of felt, the same color as the background, along the bottom. Sew vertical lines through the strip and background so that seven pockets are formed.

Make seven butterflies out of felt (they may be decorated with sequins, braid, rickrack, or other felt scraps for added color.) Pin these to the front of the seven pockets.

Place a bible verse for each week of the Easter season in the pockets. Insert a dowel in the top hem. See the illustration of the completed project.

Each Sunday the students will pin a butterfly to the cross on the top of the banner and will also learn the verse for that week. Do this for the seven weeks of Easter.

Rainbow Cross

(L/U)

Materials:
- construction paper or poster paper
- scissors
- colored paper (seven colors)
- white construction paper
- glue
- marking pen (optional)

Jesus' death and resurrection kept God's promises to his children. The cross is a sign of that, just as the rainbow was a sign of God's promises to Noah.

Option 1:
Completely cover a piece of construction paper or poster paper by gluing on seven curved strips of colored paper. Glue a white cross over all.

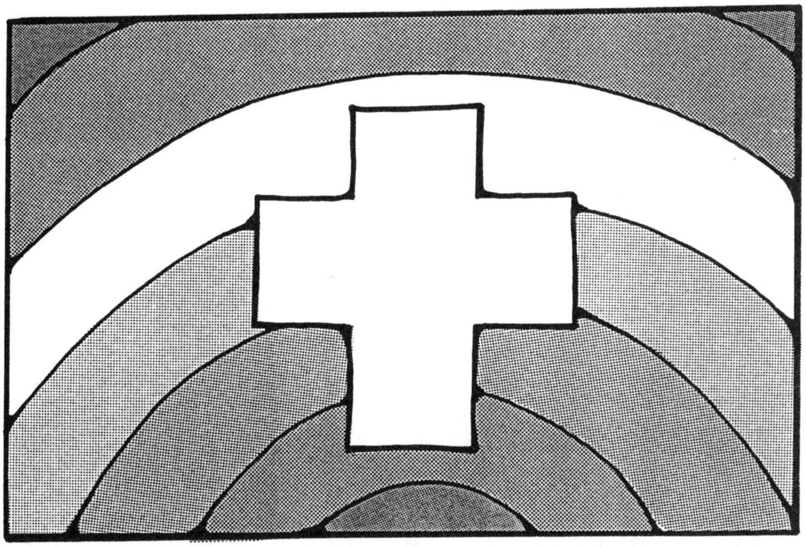

Option 2:
Cut an outline of a cross out of cardboard or poster paper. Glue seven strips of colored paper on that creating a rainbow cross. Glue the cross on a piece of white background paper.

Note:
You may add printing: "SIGN OF GOD'S PROMISE."

Easter Verse Eggs

(L/U)

Materials:
- construction paper (white or pastel)
- scissors
- marking pens
- yarn (4 to 8 inches)
- glue or stapler

Fold a piece of white or pastel-colored construction paper, about 6 by 6 inches in half. Draw an egg shape on the front so that one side of the egg runs along fold. Cut out egg, leaving folded edge uncut. Open, decorate the top layer, and write an Easter verse on the inside. See p. 90 for ideas.

Attach yarn to the top of the egg with glue or stapler. Hang in doorways or from ceiling.

Butterfly Crafts

The butterfly has long been an Easter symbol with its miraculous life cycle from cocoon to beautiful, free, new-life creature.

Following are several butterfly crafts to enjoy in the Easter season.

Silhouette Butterflies

(L/U)

Materials:
- black or purple construction paper (2 sheets)
- pencil
- scissors
- colored tissue paper scraps
- glue

Cut two large butterfly patterns (see p. 86-88) out of black or dark purple construction paper). Draw identical free-form areas on both wings and cut those areas out. Glue colored tissue paper (pastel or bright colors) behind the cut-out areas on the butterfly. Glue the two butterflies together.

Display in a window, if possible.

Flying Butterfly

(P/L/U)

Materials:
- large butterfly pattern
- scissors
- marking pens
- stapler
- tissue
- yarn or string

Cut two butterflies using the large butterfly pattern (p. 86-88). Decorate one side of each butterfly with marking pens. Staple the butterflies together, decorated sides out, around three sides, leaving the fourth side open. Stuff the butterfly with tissue, and staple the fourth side closed. Hang from the ceiling.

Butterfly Book

(L/U)

Materials:
- large butterfly pattern
- construction and lighter-weight paper
- scissors
- stapler or two brass fasteners

Trace the large butterfly pattern (see p. 86-88) onto a piece of construction paper and several sheets of lighter-weight paper, preferably colored. Cut out all the butterflies and fold them in half together. Decorate the heavier butterfly as the book cover. Staple the pages inside the cover at the book center or fasten the pages together with two brass fasteners. Draw pictures of the Easter lessons on the pages or write Easter verses. Complete this book week by week during the Easter season.

Celebration Crafts

Joy Stones

(P/L/U)

Materials:
- smooth stones
- tempera paint
- brushes

Gather smooth stones of several sizes. Paint Easter phrases and symbols on them with bright paint. Use and give away as decorations and paper weights.

Eggshell Tree

(L/U/J)

Materials:
- tree branch, anchored
- eggshells
- marking pens
- yarn or ribbon
- paper Easter symbols (optional)
- glue (optional)

Decorate clean dry eggshell halves with marking pens, or glue paper symbols of Easter onto them. Glue yarn or ribbon loop to the tops of the shells. Hang open side down from a tree branch 18 to 24 inches high, anchored in a flower pot.

Note:
The open eggs symbolize Christ's bursting from the tomb on Easter morning. These would make lovely decorations for the tables at the traditional Easter breakfast in your congregation.

Flower Signs

(L/U/J/S)

Materials:
- poster board
- scissors
- wooden stakes
- paint

Cut poster board into large flower shapes (at least 12 inches high). Decorate with Easter phrases:

He is Risen!

Happy Easter

Alleluia

Run and tell!

Attach the flowers to wooden stakes and line your church walkway with these flower signs on Easter morning.

Easter Table Runner

(L/U/S)

Materials:
- white sheet
- scissors
- waterproof marking pens

Out of a white sheet, cut a strip wide enough to lay on your worship center (or cut to fit a dining room table, if each student is to take one runner home).

Use waterproof marking pens. Decorate the runner with colorful scenes of the Easter story, phrases from Easter hymns, or happy Easter phrases.

Use the runner for class worship experiences. Every Sunday in the Christian year is a "little Easter." This will be a good reminder of that!

Easter Poster/ Banner

(U/J/S)

Materials:
Poster
- white poster board
- scissors
- colored tissue or construction paper
- glue
- white construction paper

Banner
- white felt or burlap
- scissors
- colored felt
- glue

Create a poster, using paper, or a banner, using fabric.

Cut out a path outline and glue it diagonally across the bottom as shown. Cut arches of various sizes using various colors. You can create a nice effect by staying in either all warm colors (shades of yellow, gold, orange, pink, red) or cool colors (green, glue, lilac, purple, turquoise).

Cut the angel out of white material and glue in place. Cut out the letters and glue as shown.

Creed Banner

(L/U/J)

Materials:
- used white window shade
- marking pens

Print the words of the explanation of the Second Article of the Apostles' Creed on a used white window shade. You might use different colors for the several paragraphs or for different phrases. The first letter of each sentence may be enlarged and especially decorated.

Display the banner in the classroom. This is a good tool for memory work, as it may be rolled up and then unrolled as the student recites the words.

Explanation of the Second Article

I believe that Jesus Christ—true God, Son of the Father from eternity, and true man, born of the Virgin Mary—is my Lord.

He has redeemed me, a lost and condemned person, and saved me at great cost from sin, death, and the power of the devil—not with silver or gold, but with his holy and precious blood and his innocent suffering and death.

All this he has done that I may be his own, live under him in his kingdom, and serve him in everlasting righteousness, innocence, and blessedness, just as he is risen from the dead and lives and rules eternally.

This is most certainly true.

Easter Silhouettes

(L/U/J)

Materials:
- felt (three pieces–two of one color and one of another color)
- scissors
- cardboard
- glue
- Easter symbol patterns (or original drawings)

Choose three pieces of felt, two of the same color and one in a contrasting color. A good size would be 9 by 12 inches or 11 by 14 inches. Trace several Easter symbols on a piece of thin cardboard. Cut those out, place these cardboard patterns on the one felt piece of a different color, trace, and cut out.

Arrange and glue the felt symbols onto one of the contrasting pieces of felt. Glue the piece of felt from which the symbols were cut onto the remaining felt piece, creating an effect like a picture negative.

Mount the two completed pieces on cardboard or frame them.

Joy Slides

(U/J/S)

Materials:
- old 35 mm slides
- cotton swabs
- bleach
- marking pens (fine-line)
- paper and pencil

Prepare clear slides by swabbing old 35-mm slides with cotton swabs (Q-tips, for example) soaked in household bleach. (It takes several coats before the slides become clear.)

Sketch a design for your slide on a piece of paper. When you are satisfied, draw the picture on the slide with fine-line marking pens. Allow each color to dry before using next one.

The class may prepare a slide show of abstract Easter symbols or a story from the Easter gospels.

Joy Streamers

(L/U)

Materials:
- lunch-size paper bag
- marking pens
- crepe paper
- scissors
- string (two to three feet long)
- glue or staples

Cut the bottom out of a lunch-size paper bag. Decorate the bag with marking pens using Easter phrases and/or joyous pictures or symbols. Glue colored crepe paper streamers (4 to 8 inches long) onto one end of the bag.

Knot string, attaching it to the other end of the bag in three places with glue or staples.

Run, holding the streamer out in back, for a fun, exhilarating experience!

Happy Hat

(L/U)

Materials:
- sturdy paper 12 by 18 inches
- scissors
- marking pens
- stapler
- decorations (small colorful objects)

Begin with a sheet of 12-by-18-inch white or pastel-colored paper. Cut out a half circle and decorate it with marking pens. Staple the two straight sides together to form a cone hat. Add decorations of colored paper shapes, yarn, ribbon, buttons, and other objects.

Joy Stole

(L/U)

Materials:
- felt strip (4 by 36 inches)
- colored paper or fabric for symbols
- scissors
- glue

Cut a strip of felt about 4 by 36 inches. Make and glue on paper or fabric Easter symbols. These might be worn by the children at the Sunday School worship services during the Easter Season, or they might be draped over the pew ends in the sanctuary on Pentecost Sunday to create a truly celebrative atmosphere.

They might even be made as a gift for the pastor to take on communion calls to the sick or shut-ins. The pastor might wear the stole during the sacrament and then leave it with the one being visited as a love gift from the children of the congregation.

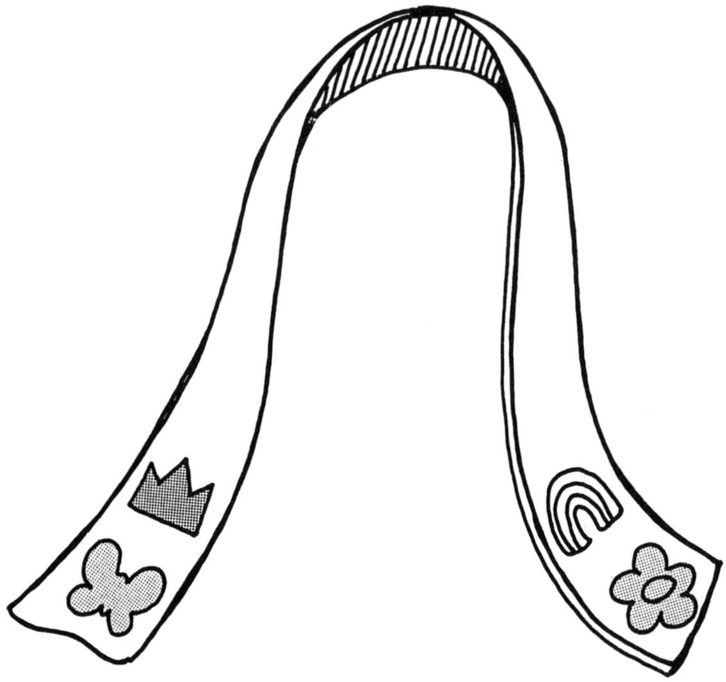

Easter Cards

Tray Print Card

(U/J)

Materials:
- styrofoam meat trays
- scissors
- sharp pencil or ball point pen
- tempera paint
- brush
- paper

Gather styrofoam meat trays of various sizes. Wash and dry them, and cut off the rounded edges to create a flat piece. Draw an Easter picture, symbol, or message on the tray using a sharp pencil or ball point pen. Use simple lines for your design.

Brush a layer of tempera paint across the tray and then place a piece of paper on top of the painted styrofoam. Rub firmly over the entire sheet of paper. Pull it off very carefully. The design will be transferred to the paper, which may now serve as your Easter card.

Add a bible verse or written message, if you wish. Sign it and send it! Repeat the process as often as you wish.

Colored Card

(L/U)

Materials:
- paper
- glue
- yarn
- scissors

Fold a sheet of paper in half and then in half again to make a French-fold card.

"Write" an Easter message (He lives!, Alleluia, Happy Easter, etc.) with glue on the front of the card. While the glue is still wet, cover the glue words with colored yarn. This creates a nice texture message. You might see the same color for the entire message or change colors with each word. Add your own message and signature inside.

Word Songs, Action Rhymes, Puzzles, and Word Games

Word Songs

Word songs are words said in rhythm without music. They bring a sense of oneness to the group doing them, a delight in the beat together, yet they do not require the skills of music reading or singing. They are within the reach of every child. They bring a sense of achievement and they're fun! These word songs are in 4/4 time. The dots indicate the beats.

Where is the Lord?

(L/U/J/S/A)

Group 1: Where is the Lord?
2: He is not here.
1: Where is the Lord?
2: He is not here.
1: Where is the Lord?
2: He is not here.
All: Run and tell the news
(whispering) (repeat)
Group 2: He is risen.
1: Allelu!
2: He is risen.
1: Allelu!
2: He is risen.
1: Allelu!
All: Run and tell the news
(soft voices) (repeat)
All: He's my Savior
Allelu!
He's my Savior
Allelu!
He's my Savior
Allelu!
Run and tell the news,
Run and tell the news
(repeat, fading to a whisper)

A Joyful Noise

(U/J/S/A)

Group 1: I can sing, I can sing, I can sing, I can sing,
(begin loudly, diminish)
Group 2: I can laugh, I can laugh, I can laugh, I can laugh
(loud to soft)
Group 1: I can shout, I can shout, I can shout, I can shout
(loud to soft)
Group 2: I can praise, I can praise, I can praise, I can praise
(loud to soft)
All: I can make a joyful noise unto God! (rest)
All: (Refrain—See p.70)

Both groups speak
at the same time

Group 1	*Group 2*
I can make a joyful noise unto God, Allelu!	I can sing, I can sing, I can sing, Allelu!
I can make a joyful noise unto God, Allelu!	I can laugh, I can laugh, I can laugh, Allelu!
I can make a joyful noise unto God, Allelu!	I can shout, I can shout, I can shout, Allelu!
I can make a joyful noise unto God, Allelu!	I can praise, I can praise, I can praise, Allelu!

Refrain: All together
Allelu, Allelu, Allelu, (brush, brush)
(brushing hands together)
Allelu, Allelu, Allelu, (snap, snap)
(snapping fingers)
Allelu, Allelu, Allelu, (clap, clap)
(clapping hands)
Alleluia! (rest, rest, rest)
(raise arms over head)

Action Rhymes

Just say the words and perform the actions indicated.

Joy Jump

(P/L)

(jump on each line—what a miracle, after all!)

Jump for joy!
Big surprise!
I just can't believe my eyes!
That big stone is rolled away!
Jump for joy this Easter day!

Body Joy

(P/L)

Put your fingers up
Put your fingers down
Put your fingers out
And give an Easter snap.
(snap your fingers)

Put your foot way up
Put your foot way down
Put your foot way out
And give an Easter tap.
(tap your toes)

Put your arms way up
Put your arms way down
Put your arms way out
And give an Easter clap!
(clap your hands together)

Easter Secret

(P/L/U)

All: It's no secret
(shake head "no," move pointer finger back and forth)
Shout it out! Shout it out!
(lean to left, hands cupped at mouth)
Tell the news, Mary, all about! *(remain in above position)*

It's no secret
(see line 1)
Shout it out! Shout it out!
(lean to right, hands cupped at mouth)
Tell the news, Peter, all about! *(remain as above)*

It's no secret
(see line 1)
Shout it out! Shout it out!
(lean forward, hands cupped at mouth)
Tell the news, *(a child's name)*, all about! *(keep that position)*

Teacher and *(named child)*: He is risen!

Whole class: He is risen, indeed!

Easter Music

I Can Sing

Sharon Lee

(L/U/J/S/A)

Easy Easter Song

(P/L)

(tune: Here we go 'round the Mulberry bush)

This is the stone that was rolled away, rolled away, rolled away,
This is the stone that was rolled away
When Jesus rose on Easter.

This is the angel who said, "He's gone," said, "He's gone," said, "He's gone,"
This is the angel who said, "He's gone,"
When Jesus rose on Easter.

This is the woman who ran to tell, ran to tell, ran to tell,
This is the woman who ran to tell,
When Jesus rose on Easter.

Puzzles and Word Games

Disciple Puzzle

(U/J/S/A)

Identify the 11 disciples who were with Jesus after he rose from the dead. Fit them in their proper spots so each is used once.

_ _ _ _ R

_ _ _ _ _ E _

_ _ _ _ S

_ _ _ _ _ _ U _

_ _ _ R _ _

_ _ R _ _ _ _ _ _ _ _

_ _ _ E _

J E S U S C H R I S T

T _ _ _ _ _

_ _ I _ _ _

_ O _ _

_ _ _ _ N

Easter Word Puzzle

(U/J/S/A)

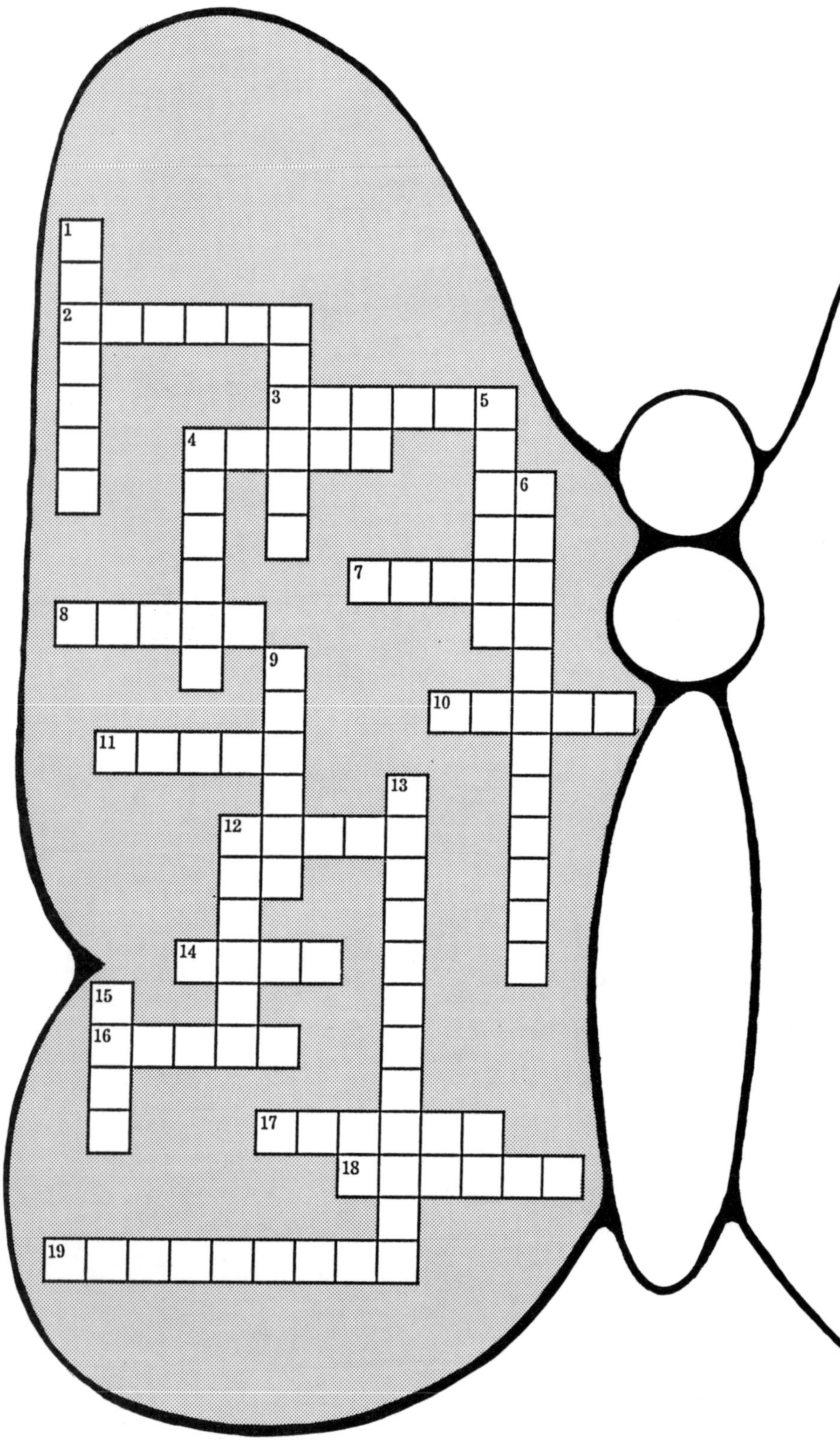

DOWN

1. The promised ___________
3. Burial place
4. The women brought this
5. First day of the week
6. The Easter miracle
9. Highest Christian Festival
12. He washed his hands of it all
13. Death on a cross
15. Sacrificial ___________

ACROSS

2. Redeemer
3. He couldn't believe it
4. It was gone!
7. He betrayed a friend
8. The body was wrapped in this
10. ___________ day of the week
11. He died for me!
12. He wept when the cock crowed
14. She first saw him that morning
16. He was there, instead.
17. Jesus, the ___________
18. It carried a king
19. A burial cave

Disciple Puzzle (Key)

```
      PeteR
     MatthEw
      JameS
    ThaddeUs
       AndRew
        BaRtholomew
       JamEs
    JESUS CHRIST
          Thomas
        PhIlip
         JOhn
      SimoN
```

Easter Word Puzzle (Key)

Down	*Across*
1 Messiah	2 Savior
3 Tomb	3 Thomas
4 Spices	4 Stone
5 Sunday	7 Judas
6 Resurrection	8 Linen
9 Easter	10 First
12 Pilate	11 Jesus
13 Crucifixion	12 Peter
15 Lamb	14 Mary
	16 Angel
	17 Christ
	18 Donkey
	19 Sepulchre

Word Add-Ons

(U/J/S)

This is a creative writing experience for the gifted student or the early arrival. It is also good as a mind-stretcher for all the children. Have plenty of graph paper on hand.

The student will write a word related to the unit being studied (start either across or down). Use the last letter of that word to begin another word going in the other direction. Continue to the end of the paper.

Examples:

```
S
T
O
N
EASTER
     E
     S
     U
     R
     R
     E
     C
     TOMB
        R
        E
        A
        D
```

```
JESUS
    A
    V
    I
    O
    REDEEM
         E
         S
         S
         I
         A
         HOSANNA
```

Hidden Easter Message

(L/U)

Materials:
- white construction paper
- white or yellow crayon
- black tempera paint and brush

This is a good lead-in for the lesson on the surprise of the Easter story. Write an Easter good news sentence or a bible verse on a card or sheet of white construction paper with a white or yellow crayon. Brush over it with black paint—the message will be revealed!

Easter News

(L/U/J)

Materials:
- paper
- newspaper
- scissors
- glue

Think up a good Easter story headline. Cut letters and/or words out of a newspaper to create your headline. Glue them on a blank piece of paper and display in your classroom.

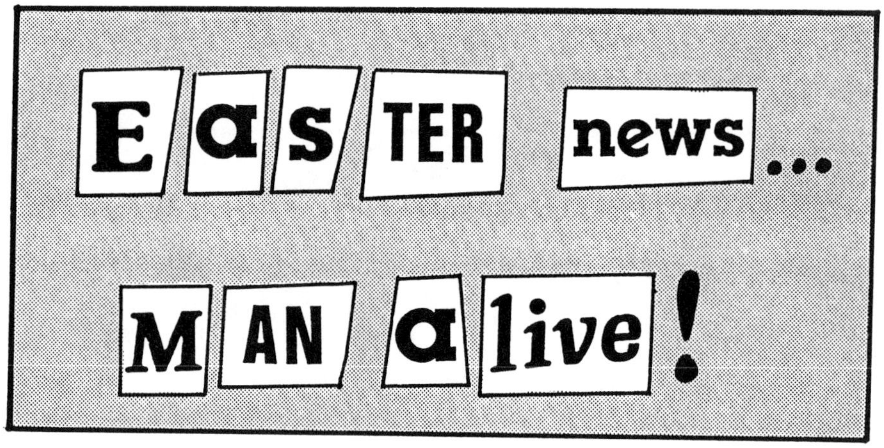

Easter Story Scramble

(U/J)

Materials:
- paper
- typewriter or pen
- scissors
- an envelope for each student
- bibles

Print the Easter story (Mt. 28:1-10) onto a piece of paper, beginning each verse on a new line and leaving space between the verses. Do not include any verse numbers.

Cut each sheet up so that each verse is on a piece of paper by itself. Mix the verses up and place all the pieces into an envelope. You might make several copies of the story and give one scrambled version to each student.

The children will try to arrange the verses in the correct order. They may then check their work in the bible.

A good memory-learning technique!

Scrambled Eggs— a quiet game

(P/L/U)

Materials:
- colored paper
- scissors
- envelopes

Make several Easter eggs out of paper. Use one color for all as a real challenge or use a different color for each egg for younger children or as an easier activity.

Cut each egg into two pieces, making one wavy-line cut. Scramble the egg parts, mixing them all up. The students will then try to match the right pieces together as quickly as possible, creating whole eggs again.

A little healthy competition may be introduced if each student keeps a timed record on him/herself, and seeks to improve his/her own speed or works against the time of other students.

This is a good, challenging activity for the early bird into the classroom or for the gifted child who finishes other tasks early.

Hope Search

(L/U/J)

Easter is the season of hope for Christians everywhere. How many times can you find the word "hope" in this word square?

h o p e h o p
o p e h o p e
p e h o p e h
e h o p e h o
h o p e h o p
o p e h o p e

Note:
The teacher may put this on the board or on poster paper as a coming-in activity or for fast workers who finish other projects quickly.

Go Quickly and Tell (An Easter Race)

(P/L/U)

Divide the group into two even teams (an extra student might be the starter and judge). Each team will form a line at the starting place. A finish line 12 to 30 feet away, depending on the available space, will be designated.

At the starting signal, the first person on each team will race to the finish line, turn and hold one hand up to signal the next teammate to run. When the second person reaches the finish line, he or she will whisper to the first, "He is risen!," turn and raise a hand for the next runner on that team.

Each subsequent player will follow in turn, saying "He is risen!" at the finish line to previous runner.

The first team finished is the winner!

Easter Maze

Help Mary find the disciples to tell her good news.

(L/U/J)

Cooking Activities

EASTER MORNING CINNAMON PUFFS

1 loaf frozen bread dough, thawed
¼ cup butter or margarine, melted
½ cup sugar
1 tsp. cinnamon

Cut dough into 12 to 16 pieces. Form into balls. Dip each one into the melted butter, then into the sugar/cinnamon mixture.

Place each puff in greased cup of muffin pan. Let rise about 45 minutes to 1 hour, until doubled.

Bake in 375° oven for 20 to 25 minutes. Remove from pan and serve warm. (12 to 16 puffs)

EASTER PATH COOKIES

2 sticks butter or margarine (½ lb.)
1 cup light brown sugar
1 cup chopped nuts
graham crackers

Use a cookie sheet with sides. Fill the bottom of the cookie sheet with a layer of whole graham crackers. Melt butter, add sugar. Boil just 2 minutes.

Remove from heat and stir in nuts. Pour mixture over the graham-cracker layer. Bake in a 350° oven for just 10 minutes. Immediately cut into thin bars. (30 to 40 bars)

MINI-CAKES

¼ cup butter or margarine
1 cup brown sugar
½ pint whipping cream
40 graham crackers, crushed
12 oz. miniature chocolate chips
1 to 2 cups fine chopped nuts (optional)

Mix the ingredients in order. Fill small paper cups about three-quarters full and set them on a baking sheet. Bake in 375° oven for 10 minutes. May be frosted, but not necessary.

CONE CAKES

Cake mix (devil's food or other chocolate)
30 to 34 flat-bottomed ice cream cones
frosting mix or can of frosting
jelly beans

Make cake batter as directed on package. Pour batter into ice cream cones, barely filling half full. Place cones on a baking sheet or in large cake pans so they are steady. Bake in 350° oven for 15 to 18 minutes. Cool. (30 to 34 cakes)

Frost with frosting and top with several colorful jelly beans. A nice treat some Sunday morning during the Easter season!

Part Three
Resources

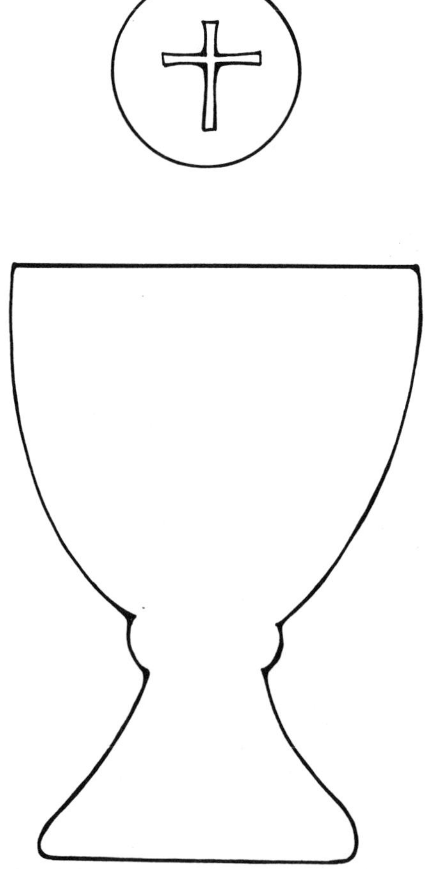

Patterns
Crosses

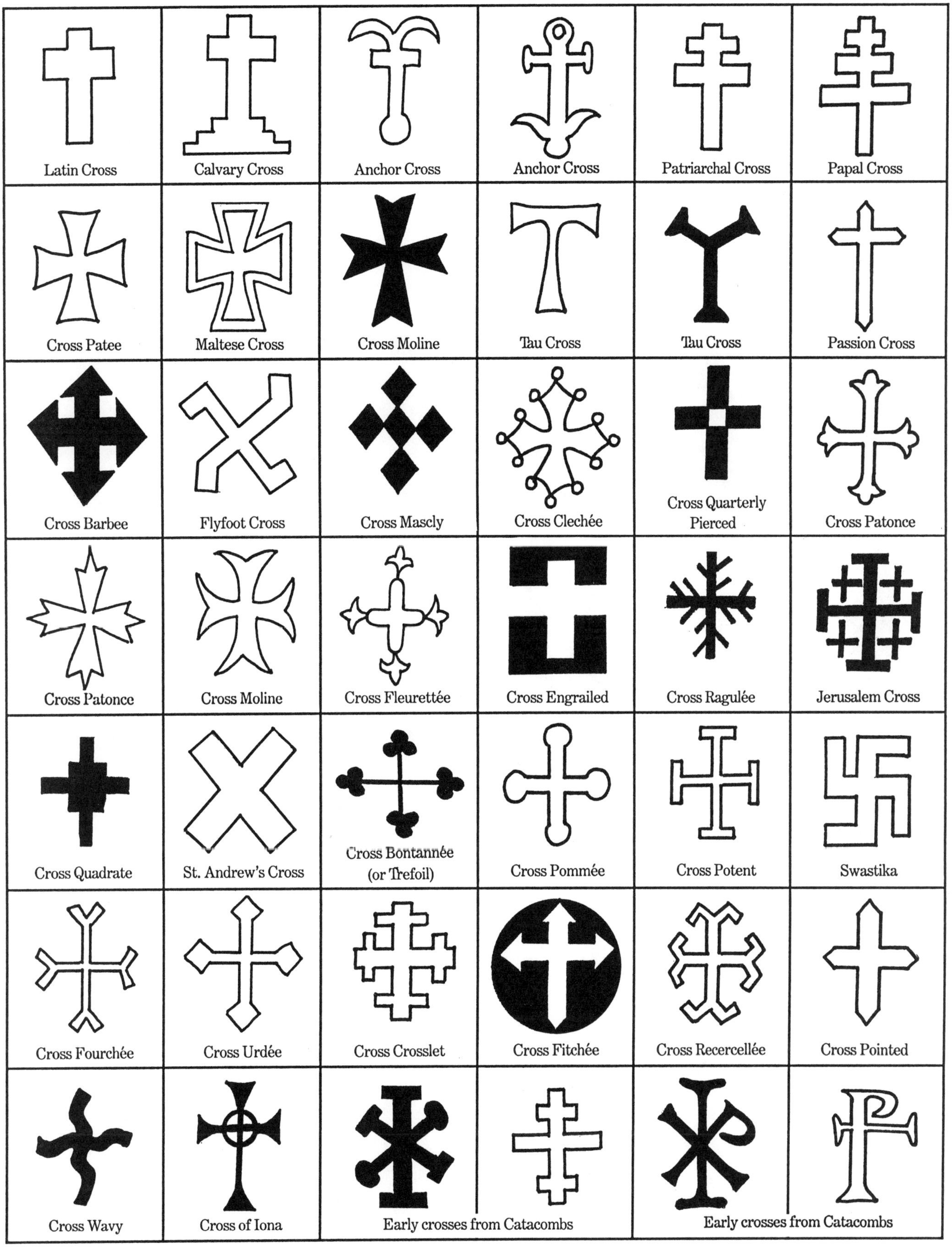

Chalice and Bread Patterns

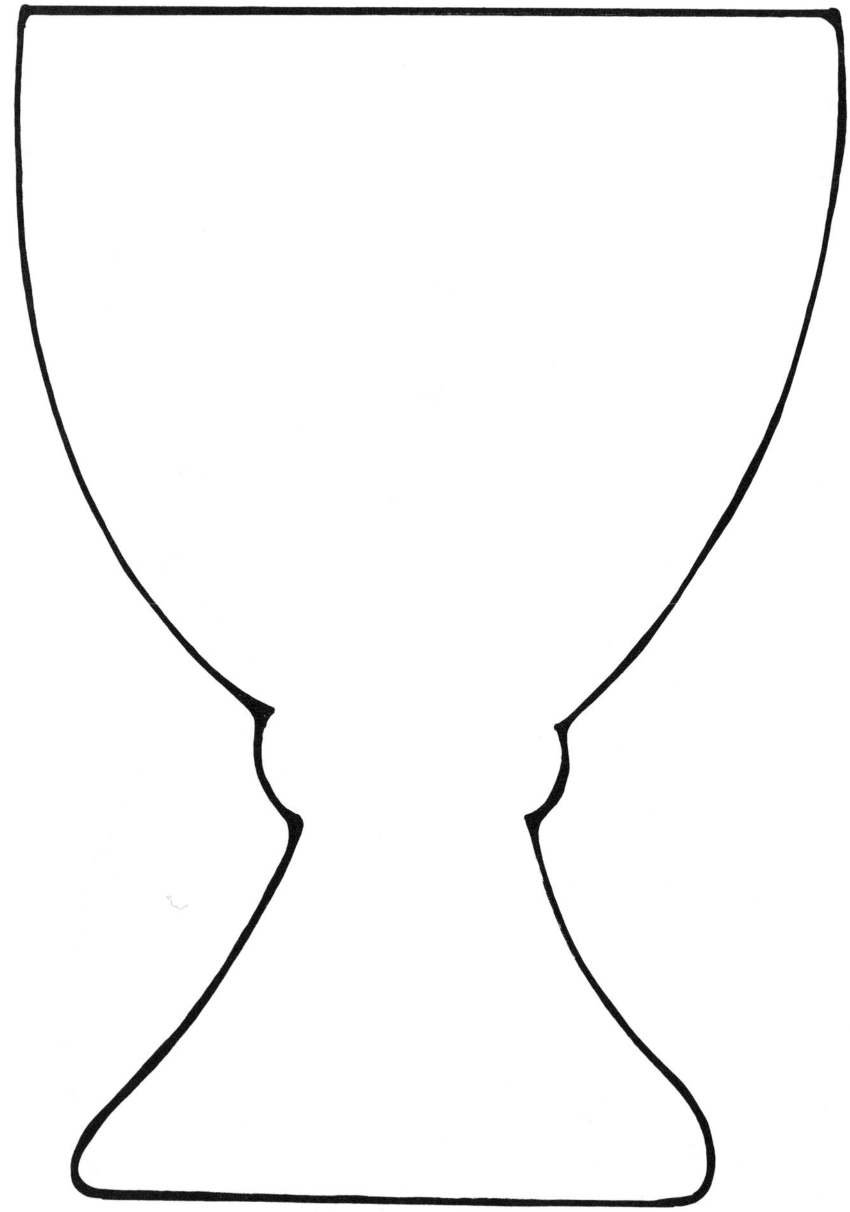

Easter Bells Pattern

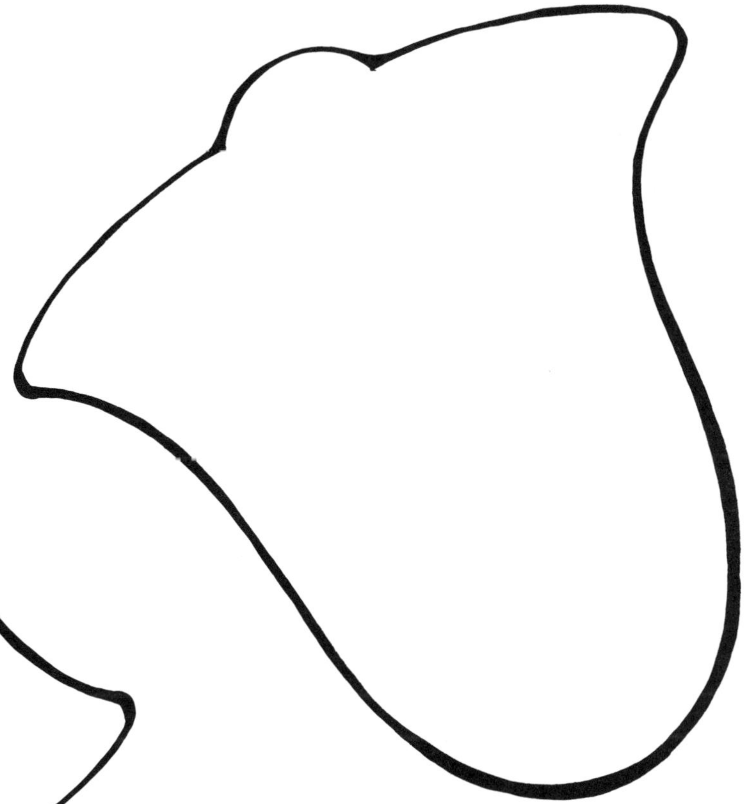

Butterfly Patterns

A Beautiful Butterflies Picture

Butterfly Patterns

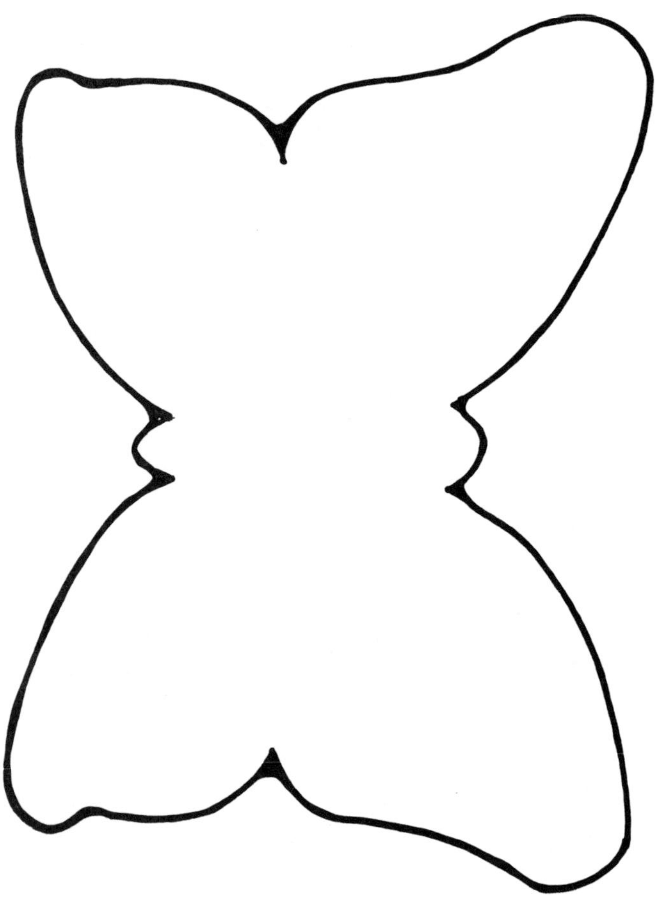

Large Butterfly Pattern

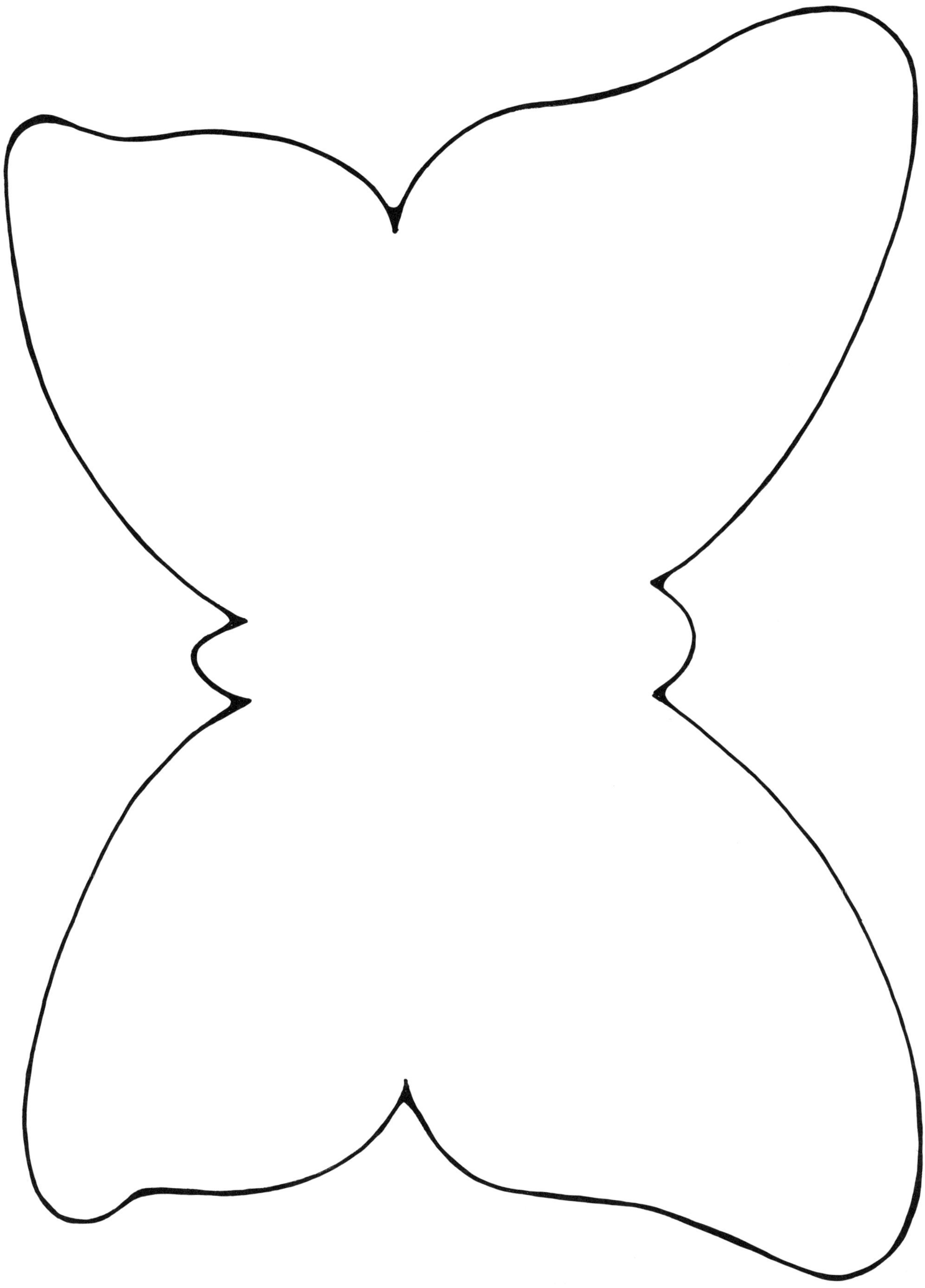

Still More Butterfly Patterns

The Events of Holy Week

SUNDAY	Jesus enters Jerusalem to cheers of the crowds waving palm branches.	Mt. 21:1-11, Mark 11:1-11, Luke 19:29-44, John 12:12-19
MONDAY	Jesus cleanses the Temple.	Mt. 21:12-17, Luke 19:45-48, Mark 11:15-19
TUESDAY	Jesus teaches in the Temple and on the Mount of Olives.	Mt. 21-24, Luke 20-21, Mark 12-13
THURSDAY	The Last Supper.	Mt. 26:17-35, Mark 14:12-16, Luke 22:1-38
	Jesus' prayers in Gethsemane.	Mt. 26:36-46, Mark 14:32-42, Luke 22:39-46
FRIDAY	The betrayal and arrest of Jesus (Jesus before Pilate and Caiphas).	John 18:1-11, Luke 22:47-53, Mark 14:43-52, Mt. 26:47-56
	The crucifixion.	Mt. 26:57-27:66, Mark 14:53-15:57, Luke 22:54-23:56, John 18-19
SUNDAY	*The resurrection.*	Mt. 28:1-10, Mark 16, Luke 24:1-12, John 20

The Seven Last Words of Christ

1. "Father, forgive them for they know not what they do." Luke 23:34.
2. "Truly I say to you, today you will be with me in Paradise." Luke 23:43.
3. "Woman, behold your son." "Behold, your mother." John 19:26-27.
4. "My God, my God, why hast thou forsaken me?" Mt. 27:46, Mk. 15:34.
5. "I thirst." John 19:28.
6. "Father, into thy hands I commit my spirit." Luke 23:46.
7. "It is finished." John 19:30.

Index of Scripture by Theme

The Last Supper
Matthew 26:17-35
Mark 14:12-26

Jesus' Prayers in Gethsemane
Matthew 26:36-46
Mark 14:32-42
Luke 22:39-46

The Betrayal and Arrest
Matthew 26:47-56
Mark 14:47-53
Luke 22:43-51
John 18:1-12

Peter's Denial
Matthew 26:69-75
Mark 14:66-72
Luke 22:54-62
John 18:15-18 and 25-27

Jesus Before the High Priests
Matthew 26:57-67 and 27:1-10
Mark 14:53-65
Luke 22:63-71
John 18:13-14 and 19-24

Jesus Before Pilate
Matthew 27:11-31
Mark 15:1-20
Luke 23:1-25
John 18:28-19:16

Good Friday — The Crucifixion
Matthew 27:32-56
Mark: 15:21-41
Luke 25:36-49
John 19:17-37

The Burial of Jesus
Matthew 27:57-66
Mark 15:42-47
Luke 23:50-56
John 19:38-42

Easter
Matthew 28:1-15
Mark 16:1-8
Luke 24:1-53
John 20:1-31

These verses refer to Jesus' Passion and Resurrection, though they are not part of the Holy Week gospel accounts. You may wish to use some of these passages in various activities in *Hosanna!* or simply for meditation.

LENT-RELATED SCRIPTURE
Isa 53:2-6
John 3:16
John 1:29
1 John 1:7
Zech. 9:9-10
Acts 2:36
2 Cor. 13:4
Gal. 2:20a
Eph. 2:13
1 Cor. 15:3
Phil. 2:5-8
Gal. 4:4-5
1 Cor. 10:16-17
Rev. 7:17

EASTER-RELATED SCRIPTURE
2 Cor. 5:17
John 11:25-26
1 Cor. 15:22
1 Cor. 15:57
Eph. 2:8
Rom. 6:3-5
1 Peter 1:8
1 Cor. 5:8
1 Cor. 15:3-7